Airlie Hall
Club Maker Series

AUCHTERLONIE

"Hand-Made Clubs"

Peter Georgiady

Foreword   Introduction

Renton Laidlaw   Keith Auchterlonie

AIRLIE HALL PRESS

KERNERSVILLE
NORTH CAROLINA

ISBN 1-886752-22-2

Layout by AHP Services

Manufactured in the United States of America

Produced by Battleground Printing & Publishing Company

Published and distributed by

AIRLIE HALL PRESS
PO Box 981
Kernersville, NC 27285
airliehall@earthlink.net

To my immediate family,

my greater golf family

and to the town of St. Andrews

For their help in research and use of photos:

Keith Auchterlonie, the late Eric Auchterlonie
and the Auchterlonie family archives

Jim Craffey, Blake Clark, Neil Crafter, Dick Durran,
Curt Fredrixon, David Hamilton, Roger Hill, Jim Horsfield,
Barry Leithhead, Ralph Livingston III, Sid Matthew,
Chuck McMullin, Tom Mitchell, Liz Pook, Joe Reisterer,
Lou Rhett, John Sherwood, Ron Stewart,
Richard Walker, Gary Wiren

Martin Kavanaugh II at The PGA Golf History center
The USGA Library with special assistance
from Patty Moran and Rand Jerris

*Cover Graphics: Foreground—The D. & W. Auchterlonie shop
with club making staff lined up in front, 1911.
Background—The new Tom Auchterlonie shop at Golf Place,
1935.*

Peter Georgiady

4

Foreword

As a Scot I was born with a natural love of and respect for the game of golf. It is in-bred in us all. We don't all play but somehow we all seem to know what it is all about. Few would admit to not liking the game. That would be sacrilege. I know the Chinese claim their emperors were playing a similar game centuries before we did; I am aware that the Romans played a type of golf between visits to the Coliseum and that the Dutch on their iced-over canals in the winter hit a hard object with a stick towards holes they had made with pick-axes in the ice, but the game, as we know it today, originated in Scotland.

Somehow it encapsulates the very nature of the Scottish character. To be a good golfer you need to be hugely determined yet massively controlled on the course. You require tiger-like aggression on the one hand but saintly patience and reserve at other times. The Scots are similar in character – dour and reserved at one moment, extrovert and noisy at another but the package remains solidly agreeable. Golf can be frustrating but also gloriously rewarding. The game tests a player's limit of endurance as

5

he or she tries to hit top form but above all it is a game in which a sense of humour in circumstances where there is little to enjoy or laugh about, is essential. The Scots, although some might dispute this, do have a sense of humour (too often deeply hidden but there nevertheless). In short golf is the ultimate, the complete test of a player's honesty and integrity and dedication to stick at it in often the most horrendous weather, which would ground even the toughest seagull.

Take all the good points about golf and all the bad – mix all the ingredients together, transfer them to wind swept links, and you have discovered all that is wonderful and frustrating about not just the game but we proud Scots – proud of our country's mountains and glens, its hundreds of carefully blended whiskies, and for introducing the game of golf to the world….yes, the world. Scots have always been great travellers and wherever they have landed and irrespective of the alien landscape or harsh climate one of the first things they always did was build a golf course. Golf after all was in their blood. In Scotland golf is a religion.

St Andrews is the home of the game and the famous Old Course stretching out towards the River Eden estuary is its shrine. Everyone with a bag of clubs and balls wants to play there at least once in his or her lifetime to experience the subtleties of links golf on an historic stretch of coastline that has tested the best golfers for centuries. No architect designed the Old Course - it just developed gradually with today's bunkers sited in natural dips and hollows where sheep once sheltered from the icy north wind that still turns the course into a diploma examination that even Tiger Woods finds demanding.

St Andrews is a place where you can walk and play on the

very turf the millionaire jet-setting superstars of today play, but also rub shoulders (metaphorically at least) with the ghosts of the past – the great golfers who used hickory sticks and gutta percha balls to shoot scores which defy belief on a course much less well manicured than it is today. Arguably the golfers who were going round the Old Course in the 70's in the 19th and early 20th century were more skilful than the best players today who are helped so much by modern technology and superb greenkeeping. The skill of the trail-blazing Scots who turned golf into a global pastime is legendary, and such is the magic of the "auld grey toun" St Andrews that there are those visitors who come, play, and insist that they were not alone on the most famous piece of golfing real estate in the world.

I am fortunate enough to have a home close by St Andrews and one evening as the sun was setting I bumped into an American professor, a learned man who had enjoyed his game, who told me how proud he had been as he stood on that huge final green, built appropriately enough over an old burial ground, to have had the help of Old Tom Morris when lining up his putt.

He insisted it was not his imagination. He had felt the old fellow's presence. He was no fool but that is what can happen when you visit St Andrews. It may be home to Scotland's oldest University and Britain's third oldest behind Oxford and Cambridge but the town's reputation as an impressive seat of learning – Prince William chose to go there and study – is overshadowed by the dedication of the locals to the great game we all love – a mental and physical game that builds character as well as affording the opportunity for healthy exercise.

It is often said, jocularly of course, that the crafty if

7

puritanical Presbyterian Scots devised a game they had to play in driving rain and bitter winds just to give themselves the justifiable excuse to enjoy a dram or two of Scotland's national drink – whisky of course - in the warmth of the clubhouse. After suffering on the course it ensured they had no guilt feelings at the 19th. Even if it is fanciful it is, nonetheless, a good story.

That may have been the case once but by the last part of the 19th century golf had become big business in St Andrews as the then new technology made the game easier and cheaper to play and improvements in transport enabled Scottish professionals from the home of golf, from Carnoustie, just across the Firth of Tay beyond Dundee, and from East Lothian to travel across the Atlantic and bring the game gloriously to America. Much has been written about the men who left Scotland to carve out lucrative careers in the United States, shaping the future of the game there with their down-to-earth teaching methods and no-nonsense attitudes…. Well most of the time at any rate!

Much less has been chronicled about the men who stayed at home in Scotland and played their part in popularising the game. I refer to the great club makers, the innovators whose imagination and great skills when fashioning beautifully weighted clubs with their hands played as important a part in the development of golf as those golfing missionaries who sailed away to the new world. In this respect you think immediately of the famous St Andrews golfing families – the Philps, the Forgans, the Morrises and the Auchterlonies. Old Tom Morris is a legendary figure and his son young Tom who died aged just 25 of - they say - a broken heart following the death of his wife in childbirth - are equally honoured and respected. Their story is well enough known but the part the

Auchterlonies played in the development of the game is not – until now, that is, thanks to this new book by another golfing aficionado and author whose affection for golf is not in question.

The story of the Auchterlonie family, two members of which — Willie and, later, his son Laurie — would, like Old Tom Morris before them, be honoured with the post of honorary professional to the Royal and Ancient Golf Club of St Andrews – is fascinating and not without intrigue. Willie was an Open winner and his brother Laurie, while staying in America, was an early winner of the US Open but although the Auchterlonie boys were all good golfers it was as club makers that the really made their name. The family's connection with golf stretches all the way back to 1768. Later, when club-making became as profitable as or even more financially rewarding than plumbing, plastering or working long hours as a farm labourer, the Auchterlonies were ready to take advantage.

The early realisation that, as the game increased in popularity more clubs, all of them then hand-made from specially selected wood, would be required was the inspirational springboard the Auchterlonies needed to become one of the largest of a series of well-known club makers in the Kingdom of Fife. The family not only made high-quality clubs, much sought after today by antique dealers and collectors, they were inventors also. New designs for putters and short game irons hit the market thanks to the ingenuity of the Auchterlonies - Tom in particular. The Registered Putting Cleek, the Holing Out Putter and, indeed, the fore-runner of the modern golfing iron were among the Auchterlonie inventions.

The reputation of the firm for superlative hand-crafted clubs was made early on and, although techniques have

9

changed dramatically, the Auchterlonie name lives on. Sales in the Auchterlonie shop on the corner of Golf Place may have diversified dramatically but it is still there – a link with a vibrant and exciting period in the development of the game even if there were squabbles, never fully explained, which affected family relationships dramatically.

The various branches of the Auchterlonie family and what they achieved in their different ways have played and continue to play an important part in the history of St Andrews and the development of golf. Some of their achievements may surprise you but there has always been a dedication to producing a quality product. The family's skills in the workshop match those of the great golfers on the course – men such as Jack Nicklaus who, unashamedly, has always rated St Andrews and the Old Course as his favourite venue. Jack did win two of his

Renton Laidlaw and the author, at The Masters, April, 2003, on the occasion of Renton being honored by the PGA of America with their award for Lifetime Achievement in Journalism.

three Open Championships there, of course.

Yet St Andrews means much more to the man voted the greatest golfer of the 20th century ahead of his own hero Bobby Jones, and Arnold Palmer, than two Open wins. The Golden Bear chose St Andrews and the Old Course for his emotional farewell in 2005. He left the scene tearful, surrounded by his family, applauded by his fellow competitors and cheered to the echo by adoring crowds yet unable to celebrate honorary citizenship.

I don't know whether Jack, like that other American gentleman, felt the presence of Old Tom Morris or Willie or Laurie Auchterlonie on that final green when he holed, significantly, his last birdie putt in a major but I do know that one of the greatest of all sportsmen has had and always will have a special feeling for the town, the course and especially the townsfolk - people such as the Auchterlonies, superb craftsmen, who over the years have, in their own distinctive way, played as important a role off the course, as Jack Nicklaus has on it.

Renton Laidlaw
Evening Standard,
London

May 2006

Peter Georgiady

Introduction

Forgan, Morris, Auchterlonie: names to quicken the pulse of any golf historian.

For me, however, as a boy growing up in 1950s St Andrews, these names and the businesses behind the names were just part of the scenery. Being able to walk into the factories and workshops, see the clubs being made, talk to the club makers, and play with the tools and machinery was commonplace. It was no more special than the view of the Golden Gate would be to a San Francisco kid or than riding on a tractor would be to a farmer's son.

I realise now, with the benefit of hindsight, how privileged I was to have been able to experience at first hand the last of the craftsmen club makers. However, because these experiences were the norm, I never thought them worthy of special note. As a result, many of these memories of mine have either been forgotten or become blurred over time.

Writing like this, I am aware that it reads as though I am describing some dim and distant past. However, these memories are less than 50 years old. In the space of not much more than a score of years, the skills of the club maker became redundant. The whole way of making golf clubs changed – the process moved from being a craft industry to a technological and manufacturing one. The end results are undoubtedly very effective, allowing lower scoring from everybody from rabbit to top professional, but the soul has gone. The club making era in Scotland has become history.

The Auchterlonies of St. Andrews: Three generations—Tom, young Keith and Eric.

Much about the game, itself, has changed, too. Right into the 1970s, we would have the leading players of the day coming in to my father's workshop to make last minute adjustments to their clubs before going out to do battle in the Open or whichever tournament was being played on the Old Course. I had my first golf lesson from Max Faulkner – a frequent visitor - not many years after his Open victory at Portrush, and other champions such as Bobby Locke always dropped in to the shop when they were competing at St Andrews. Again, this just went with

14

the territory.

Because, as the song goes "You don't know what you've got 'til it's gone*", there is a real risk that much of this history will be lost to future generations of golf enthusiasts, collectors and historians.

Therefore, I was delighted when Pete, whose scholarship and enthusiasm about club making history I so admire, wrote to me to tell me that he had chosen our family as his latest project. Although I can't claim any credit for the book you have in front of you, I have found working with Pete to be a joy. I have found out things that I didn't know about my family – both directly from Pete and by being prompted by him to look into matters that he was interested in. It's been an education for me, as well as a pleasure.

My late father, Eric, who I regarded as pre-eminently knowledgeable about these matters, wrote the foreword to one of Pete's earlier books, *Compendium of British Club Makers*. In it, he wrote: "There was so much that went on in our shop over the years. I wish I could remember it all; we just did not feel that it was important at the time. My father was a gold mine of information." My feelings echo his 100%.

If this book helps to keep alive some of the history of St Andrews club making it will, for me, have been a success.

Keith Auchterlonie

*From the song "Big Yellow Taxi," written and performed by Joni mItchell, 1970, on the Warner label.

Prologue

In September, 1971 when I set out for a year at the university of Dundee I had been playing golf for 13 years. The name St Andrews—home of golf was vaguely familiar but neither I, nor a whole lot of other Americans could probably identify its exact whereabouts. It was only after arriving at Dundee that I recognized I was virtually on the doorstep of that famous town.

My first opportunity to set foot in the Royal Burgh of St Andrews came a few days after my arrival when one of the lads, Dave Harrison, suggested we go to St Andrews for a few beers on a Saturday afternoon. He had the car so he and I along with Dave Thomas, Ian Cowie, Gary Lochhead and Steve Crook piled in and drove the twelve miles south. That trip afforded me my first glimpse of the courses and the Auchterlonie shops, conspicuous as we drove into town from the north.

Thirty-five years after that beer run, this book comes as one of life's milestones. I could say it was published at the end of a long friendship but that friendship is really not yet over and has begotten other friendships that will continue onward for many more years.

My friends know, and are probably tired of hearing, about my times in Scotland while at Dundee. I like to say those days spent among the Scots, and more importantly on their golf courses, were my apotheosis. I was transformed from someone who merely went out and played golf to, as P.G. Wodehouse phrased it, "a golfer of spirit," schooled in the history, lore and mystic rites of the Royal and Ancient game.

During that Scottish sojourn two very important figures

emerged. Mr. Doug Glassey was the licensed grocer that just happened to have the brand of brown ale I most appreciated. As my self-appointed host, he made it his duty to ensure I played golf—not just golf but golf played on Scotland's greatest courses—during my time in Dundee. Doug gave me my first antique golf club on a return trip to Dundee and St Andrews in 1975. The other was Mr. Eric Auchterlonie, proprietor of the golf shop at the corner of Pilmour Links and Golf Place in St Andrews. Eric served as an early mentor once I had realized that the history of golf, and particularly golf club makers, was a field of knowledge I wanted to pursue.

It would be difficult to imagine anyone coming to St Andrews and not seeing the Tom Auchterlonie shop. It is almost as difficult to comprehend the visitor not stopping in, if only to browse. As student visitors, Dave Thomas and I popped in on every trip to the town links, usually to purchase a handful of individually wrapped 1.62 size balls we would later donate to the thick gorse or the waist-high 'elephant grass' on those parts of the courses one was not supposed to frequent. And it was on one of those stops that I struck up my first meaningful conversation with the old gentleman I would later learn was not Tom but Tom's son, Eric. In time he had decorated the ceiling of the shop with wood shaft clubs from his trove of old stuff. Of particular interest was the rut iron and I, like every other novice to the history of golf equipment, found it remarkable that a club had actually been crafted specifically to extricate the ball from a wagon rut on a golf course. From that day forward, Eric and I had a running dialogue on clubs, history, and the philosophy behind the game of a century ago.

In later years, when I returned on brief golf holidays, we'd talk about old clubs and makers each day. When I stopped

17

in the next morning to bid him a quick hello, he'd have clubs to show me produced by the makers we had discussed the day before. Over the evening, Eric would rummage around his store room to find examples of stuff we had just talked about. He'd tell me about "Jimmy Sherlock" or "Davey Anderson" as if they had just been through the door to his shop a day or two earlier. Eric never hid his contempt for that town rogue, R.B. "Buff" Wilson.

It remains a great point of contention in my life whether I was wrong to not sit in the shop and continue those conversations at length—at the expense of playing the Old or the New—or whether the on-course experiences carried appropriate vindication for the time spent. (Throwing further weight toward the philosophical argument that playing 'the golf' was the acceptable choice, a round on the Old was only a pound, the New was 60p., the Eden 40p., and a glorious 18 holes on the Jubilee was a scant 35p. Off-season, during the university term, there was hardly ever a wait to go off.)

A further high spot in our relationship was a visit in 1982 with my three-year-old son Bryan. During that trip, I saw a Tom Auchterlonie signature model juvenile sand iron hanging on the showroom wall. I commissioned one to be assembled and when I made my daily call the next morning, Eric himself was just sliding the Golf Pride grip on the shaft. He had cut the club to be ready for Bryan when he reached a size where the club's balance was proper for a young man of about six years old. Because the club's loft got the ball airborne very quickly, it was the first club young Bryan learned to hit out of the back yard grass back home in Ohio.

Our last meeting was bittersweet. The meeting itself was

The exterior of the shop from Golf Place as it appeared in 1982.

fine—several hours in the parlor at the home of his retirement in nearby Pitscottie. But we had been in town for almost a week and a bad cold had kept Eric confined to bed until the afternoon of our last day. I spent a full afternoon in his parlor taping our entire conversation on a hand held recorder.

A year later, as I was assembling all the fragments that collectively made *The Compendium of British Club Makers*, I asked Eric to write the foreword and he agreed. He did the work but before the book made it into print he passed away. His son Keith contacted me and assisted by adding a postscript to his father's foreword, and then stayed in long-distance touch with me. Thirteen years later we embarked on this project.

I wrote a brief obituary for Eric Auchterlonie in USGA's *Golf Journal*, a paragraph from which I include here, to recognize the end of an era, to observe the conclusion of one family's special history.

> *A golf club maker in St Andrews for almost 60 years,*
> *Eric Auchterlonie was probably the last living member*
> *of any of the major club making families who worked*
> *during the hickory shafted era. Specializing in hand*
> *made clubs, the Auchterlonie name was synonymous*
> *with the highest quality available.*

Golf Journal, *September, 1992*

One of the items Eric once told me helps put the title of this book into perspective. He lamented the coming of the non-wood shaft to golf manufacture, because that was precisely what it had become: manufacture. Metal shafts made golf clubs lose their individuality. They negated the skill and craftsmanship the best club makers instilled in their product and cost the jobs of hundreds of club making staff in the shops of the large club makers. Even before the advent of tubular metal shafts, at a time when mass production methods were creeping into the wood shaft club making business, the Auchterlonies promoted their firm as one that produced "Hand-Made Clubs."

Wm Auchterlonie

Laurie Auchterlonie

Tom Auchterlonie

Top: Golf on the Old Course, circa 1900, from a postcard of the day.

Bottom: A similar view from a card mailed in 1906.

22

The Auchterlonies of St Andrews

Hugh Philp, legendary St Andrews club maker, was the son of an agricultural laborer. Robert Forgan's father was harbor master of Pittenweem, down the coast from St Andrews. Tom Morris's father was, according to W.W. Tulloch, a hand weaver in St Andrews. It should be no surprise that the patriarch of the several Auchterlonies who entered the ranks of club makers was also not a club maker himself. David Auchterlonie was a master plumber. While the Patricks of Leven and the McEwans, Dunns and Parks of Musselburgh had more club making experience in their lineage, the St Andrews families began later. David Auchterlonie own Uncle David represented the proletariat nature of Scottish golf—he was a founding member of the St Andrews Mechanics Golf Club at its inception in 1843. Later (1851) it became the St Andrews Golf Club to which his grand-nephews would also belong.

The Auchterlonie family line can be traced as far back as 1634 and located in the village of Ceres, Fife. For golf purposes the family presene in St Andrews begins with the grandfather of the elder David Auchterlonie, who was born in 1768, so the family was resident in the harbor town for almost a century by the time the first of the six brothers was born.

23

David and Margaret Auchterlonie had a family comprised of six sons and two daughters (a third daughter died in infancy). Young David was born in 1865 and William in 1872. They would be the offspring who learned the craft then started the Auchterlonie club making business. The first born child, James, continued in his father's footsteps as a plumber but was a fine golfer in his off hours. The third child, Joseph, began his working life as a plasterer but eventually turned to club making, working for brothers David and Willie. Following Joe were David, Lawrence, Sarah, Willie and Tom. Lawrence* also worked as a club maker but emigrated to America to secure his fame. Tom was the youngest, born in 1879. He also worked for David and Willie, eventually starting the second of the family's golf club business in town. Daughter Ann was the second child behind James and apparently never married, remaining at home to care for her parents. Daughter Sarah married a club maker named Dick Brown.

Precisely when David went to work at Robert Forgan's firm is not clear but since he was seven years older than Willie, it's a good bet he was there first and possibly helped secure a place for Willie later. Willie began his apprenticeship with Forgan's in 1887 when he was 15 years old. He had, at that point, been playing golf his entire life. As a young child he and his brothers would hit bits of cork with a stick using lampposts as targets, later he fashioned his own primitive clubs from pieces of scrap wood. Apprenticing in his mid-teens, it is interesting to

* Formal records indicate that Laurie's given name was Lawrence, spelled with a 'w.' Throughout most of his professional life, golf records and verbiage in golf periodicals referred to him as Laurie or Laurence. Since sources like *The Golfer*, quoted several times in this volume, use the Laurence spelling, it is used herein as well.

note that he was already a skillful golfer yet he owned only two clubs—a wooden play club and an iron cleek. At Forgan's, he was employed by the largest club making firm in the world at that time.

A photo of Forgan's staff in *Golf in the Making*, by David Stirk and Ian Henderson, shows David and Willie (as well as Andrew Crosthwaite) in a group of 35 Forgan employees. That photo is listed as being the staff of 1895 however that date may easily be a two years later than when the photo was taken since the brothers and Andrew were working in their own newly founded shop in late 1893.

The Auchterlonie boys belonged to the St Andrews Golf Club, established 1843. *The Golfer* (July 29, 1896) reported on the strength of the Club's team by profiling all the exceptional amateur golfers in the club's membership.

> *LAURENCE AUCHTERLONIE is a player of whom it is paradoxically said that no man could beat if he wouldn't beat himself. Laurie just misses greatness through inability to study self-control as well as the game. His club played 23 score competitions last year. Laurie competed in 17 of these, his average round being 83 1/2. His lowest round was 75, which, in a score competition, stands as the record on St Andrews Links. He has been a frequent medal winner, while, as a partner with P. C. Anderson, he won the Times Trophy at Leven. He also won the Nairn Amateur Cup last year, and, being yet young, we may confidently look forward to his being yet crowned with higher laurels.*

25

This photograph of the St. Andrews Golf Club was taken in 1894 or very early 1895. Four of the six Auchterlonie brothers are pictured. Willie was classed as a professional at this time and Tom was probably still in school. Other members of note are George Lorimer, who worked in the Auchterlonie & Crosthwaite shop with David and Willie, and Jim Foulis, at Chicago Golf Club in 1895 and was the US Open champion in 1896.

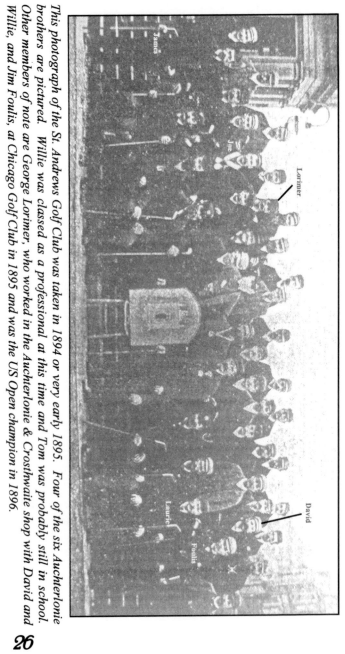

JAMES AUCHTERLONIE is the eldest of the family of that name. He is in business with his father as a plumber. That he is a very able golfer will at once be granted, and, although his business, and his duties a bandmaster of the city band, make his rounds on the links few and far between, yet he holds his own with the best.

DAVID AUCHTERLONIE of that ilk has this peculiarity-his place in a competition can almost always be fixed before starting. He has a partiality for going round with an almost invariable score of 87 or 88, which, although extremely useful in club play, just causes him to all but gain the medal.

JOSEPH AUCHTERLONIE is another of the same family. He has heights and depths in his game that are puzzling. He (like J. Robb this year) won the two scratch medals of the club successively. His scores were 82 on both occasions, and these scores established a record for medal play till lowered by P. C. Anderson. He also won the gold medal presented by the Royal and Ancient Club for competition among the local clubs.

Inclusion on that list of thumbnails was for club members that were amateurs. Willie, having won the Open (and more importantly, accepted the prize money) three years earlier, was no longer able to compete for the club as an amateur. David, was still an amateur, despite the fact he was managing the club making business. For club makers like David and Laurie Auchterlonie, the club still recognizes them as amateurs if they have not played golf for money nor caddied. In 1896 Tom Auchterlonie was still only 17-years-old and had just begun working.

27

St. Andrews Directory

Auchterlonie, Mrs Christina, 101 Market street
Auchterlonie, David, clubmaker, 3 Pilmour links
Auchterlonie, David, plumber, 9 Union street

Auchterlonie, Miss, 1 Church square
Auchterlonie, Jean, dressmaker, 101 Market street
Auchterlonie, James, plumber, 14 Melbourne place
Auchterlonie, Joseph, clubmaker, 121 North street
Auchterlonie, Thomas, clerk, 7 Park street
Auchterlonie, Thomas, plasterer, 29 Market street
Auchterlonie, Thomas K., bootmaker, 101 South street
Auchterlonie, William, clubmaker, 9 Union street

The 1909 St Andrews Directory, much like today's phone book (except few people had phones in 1909), listed residents of the town, their address and occupation. In 1909 David Auchterlonie is shown living over the Pilmour Links shop. Willie is still residing at his parents' house on Union Street, where his father also lives. Joseph was resident at 121 North Street and Tom, listed as a clerk is at the house on Park Street. The eldest of the six brothers, James, works as a plumber in his father's footsteps. Laurie was still in America. Several other Auchterlonies, related and unrelated, are also shown.

This photograph of David Auchterlonie appeared in a 1907 issue of Golf Illustrated *and is one of the very few portrait-style photos of him.*

DAVID AUCHTERLONIE, THE SENIOR PARTNER IN THE FIRM

WILLIE AUCHTERLONIE, OPEN CHAMPION IN 1893.

Willie Auchterlonie fourteen years after he won the Open Championship.

29

The 1893 Open Championship

For the Auchterlonie family, there was a single moment that literally defined their existence: the Open Championship of 1893 played at Prestwick. Prior to that contest, young Willie Auchterlonie had played in two Opens, finishing 8th in 1891. The '91 Open was played on his home course, St Andrews, and was won by Hugh Kirkaldy, also a St Andrews product. It was the last of the 36-hole events. The '92 Muirfield Open, the first of the 72-hole contests, was won by an amateur, the elegant Mr. Harold H. Hilton. Although Willie's name does not appear on the final tally sheet, it was noted he had entered. Auchterlonie's victory in 1893 changed the profile of the prodigious golfing family from talented also-rans to champions of the first order. The Open Championship was barely 30 years old yet winning was now the veritable *faît accompli* for any golfer's resume and the winner became a national hero, a household name, a merchandising icon and in young Willie's case, a meteorically rising star.

The tenor of that tournament was set when the first day's round was played in rain that every report labeled as 'torrential.' Willie was credited with besting the field through his long drives with lots of carry, essential when playing on sodden ground. The publication *The Field* wrote:

> *On the opening day it rained in the most pitiless fashion from morn till eve, and players, and whose business compelled them to be present, had a most unenviable outing for, lovely spot as the far-famed Ayrshire green of Prestwick may be on a fine summer day when the sun glints on the peaks of*

W. AUCHTERLONIE, ST. ANDREWS.
CHAMPION GOLFER, 1893.

This was one of Willie Auchterlonie's official Open Champion studio photographs taken in the days after the 1893 Tournament.

Golfing Annual
1894

Arran, we can conceive of no more dismal place when the rain drives in from the broad expanse of the Firth of Clyde. In the opinion of Tom Morris, playing in his 33rd consecutive Open, conditions were the worst ever experienced.

The *Golfing Annual* tribute to the 1893 champion, as do the accounts from other periodicals, extol Willie's growing achievements on the green leading up to his Open victory. It discounts thoughts that his win might be a 'snatch' victory and suggests that the 21-year-old was just now hitting stride. However, despite playing well and carrying the cachet of Open Champion, Auchterlonie never again came close to winning. His best effort was a fifth place

31

finish on his home course in 1905 and he actually missed the cut in 1898 by falling more than 20 strokes behind at the tournament's mid-point. That was the first Open to limit players by score after the first two rounds and it was on the Prestwick course that saw him win five years earlier. In the 20 years after Willie's victory, the Great Triumvirate—Vardon, Taylor and Braid—dominated the Open until World War I leaving little room for outsiders to assert themselves.

Late in his life, *The Scotsman* wrote of Willie,

> *But Auchterlonie was a club-maker at heart, and it was only after much coaxing by his fellow workmen [at Forgan's] that he went to the championship, and as a matter of fact, turned his back entirely on title chances and settled down to the club-making business, and he confesses to-day that he has had no regrets.*

One bit of trivia that was often recalled during Willie's lifetime, was the fact that in his final round of the first day at the Prestwick Open, he shot an 8 from the railway tracks on the first hole. A second item involving Willie's performance in the '93 Open was his choice of caddies. His clubs were carried by Harry Turpie, a fellow St. Andrean, who emigrated to the United States in 1897. But in 1895 Willie finished in a tie for 31st place—tied with Turpie, his caddie of two years before. Turpie eventually wound up as professional to the Edgewater Country Club on Chicago's north side where he schooled a young caddie named Charles Evans. Known to the world as "Chick," Evans was the first American to hold the US Open and US Amateur titles concurrently, won during the 1916 season.

In the years leading up to the year of his Open victory,

Another photo of Willie Auchterlonie, the Champion, simulating his address to the ball.

Golf (UK)
February 23, 1894

Willie played in the first four championships staged for the St Andrews-based club makers working in the firms of Forgan or Morris. The first year, he tied with Jamie Anderson but was the champion in the next three years. This tournament was his favorite but in '93, just before setting out for Prestwick's Open, he lost the Clubmaker's Medal to an upstart—Old Tom, himself, still excelling at golf and giving the youngsters a whipping at 72 years old.

Willie Auchterlonie's record in the Open Championship:

1891   St AndrewsT-8,   9 strokes behind H. Kirkaldy
1892   Muirfield, Finishing place unclear
1893   Prestwick, 1st place by 2 strokes over Mr. Laidlay
1894   Sandwich, T-23, 29 strokes behind J.H. Taylor
1895   St Andrews, T-31; 32 strokes behind Taylor; 14 strokes behind his brother Laurie (an amateur, T-13 place)
1896   Muirfield, T-12, 13 strokes behind H. Vardon
1897   Hoylake, T-18, 22 strokes behind H. Hilton
1898   Prestwick, Missed "cut"
1899   Sandwich, Missed "cut"
1900   St Andrews, 5th, 17 strokes behind J.H. Taylor
1901   Muirfield, T-29, 23 strokes behind J. Braid
1902   Hoylake, T-38, 32 strokes behind A. Herd
1903   Prestwick, T-45, 30 strokes behind H. Vardon

Auchterlonie and Crosthwaite

In the late 1880s and early 1890s, golf was growing by leaps and bounds in all of Britain and the Empire and flourishing in Fife. The old guard from Leith, Musselburgh and Edinburgh was giving way to the new epicenter—St Andrews. Through the 1870s and into the 1880s the champions from St Andrews named Kidd, Martin, Burns and Anderson showed that golf talent was steadily breeding in the Auld Grey Toun.

The firms supplying equipment to Scotland and the world were Forgan's and Morris's works. Robert White, Robert Wilson and Willie Wilson were forging iron clubs, soon to be joined by Robert Condie and Tom Stewart. David Anderson's new shop was quickly making a name for itself. Clubs were being exported to expatriates in the far-flung corners of the Empire and golf was just catching on in the United States and Canada.

David Auchterlonie probably got a job at Forgan's first, as that firm expanded to meet increasing orders, and was able to secure work for his younger brother, Willie, in 1887. They would have been taken on as apprentices to learn the trade before becoming regular workers. During that five-year period they undoubtedly made friends with another worker, Andrew Crosthwaite. Understanding the prospects of the new golf market, they made arrangements to strike out on their own in September, 1893. The firm, called Auchterlonie & Crosthwaite, initially had three employees—David, Andrew and Willie.

For a start, the firm worked alongside their father's plumber's workshop at 9 Union Street, which, in turn, was beside the family home, near the center of St Andrews.

Some time in 1894 the firm had taken up quarters in a legitimate storefront at 146 North Street, to be closer to the links and commercial traffic.

George Lorimer was an important employee. He was a highly respected club maker in St Andrews, working for Tom Morris for many years, and it was said he made some of the earliest bulgers in the late 1880s when that club was shaking up the golfing world. *Golf*, when it published thumbnail sketches of members of the St Andrews Golf Club, wrote this about Lorimer:

> *GEORGE LORIMER has never exerted himself to be a great golfer, but, as a clubmaker, he is par excellence. There are not many first-class players in the golfing world who have not gone to Geordie to get their ideas of making a club carried out.*

The Registered Approaching Cleek

Besides being the launching pad for Auchterlonie club making activity for the next 93 years, the most important contribution to golf coming from the firm of Auchterlonie and Crosthwaite was Auchterlonie's Special Registered Approaching Cleek*. The design of the Approaching Cleek was the product of Willie Auchterlonie, who applied himself mostly to club design and manufacture while David took care of much of the routine business for the firm and

---

* The differences between patenting a golf club and registering its design are numerous but not particularly important. Patenting carried with it more protection for misuse or design theft than does registering the design. However, the process takes longer to complete. Many makers opted to achieve a design copyright, it being faster and less cumbersome to be granted.

timber selection. The club was introduced in 1894 and if the Auchterlonies' advertisements were to be believed, initial sales were brisk. At some point after 1896 the great open champion James Braid used an Auchterlonie Approaching Cleek with success and espoused the musselback design, incorporating it into his own model clubs.

The term Approaching Cleek is unique for the Auchterlonie's club even though subsequent makers put out similar clubs with the same name. The shape of the blade is a low profile bar and the loft is close to a medium iron. In Scottish golf terminology, the 'lofting cleek' eventually gave way to the new name of the 'jigger.' The Approaching Cleek is not dissimilar to the jigger, a utility club with middle iron distance.

While collectors deem any patented or registered (design) club collectible, the Special Registered Approaching Cleek occupies its small spot in club making history because it is the first iron to be made in the 'musselback' shape. It was the thickening of the blade behind the sweetspot extending to the sole that made the registered design unique. The registration number is stamped on each club, pointing back to a record kept in the shop that describes the club's weight, length (of shaft), loft and lie.

AUCHTERLONIE & CROSTHWAITE
(W. AUCHTERLONIE, Open Champion 1893),
Golf Club and Ball Makers,
146 NORTH STREET, ST ANDREWS.

Auchterlonie's SPECIAL REGISTERED
APPROACHING CLEEK kept in Stock.

An early advertisement for the firm of Auchterlonie and Crosthwaite, now a little more than a year old, from The Golfer, *November 24, 1894.*

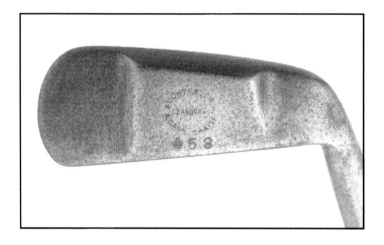

The Registered Approaching Cleek was the first club to add a 'chunk' of weight behind the sweetspot. Each club was marked with a sequence, or manufacturing number. This club was number 458 to be produced. It has the standard Auchterlonie and Crosthwaite mark but carries no fern frond cleek marks from the Condie forge. In the parlance of the day, the approaching cleek was an iron with a cleek shaped blade but an approaching loft, about the angle of a mashie. (More Approaching Cleeks on pages 64-65)

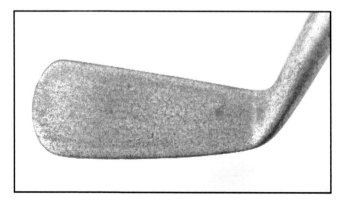

Auchterlonie & Crosthwaite Clubs

Clubs made by the firm of Auchterlonie and Crosthwaite are relatively scarce. They date from the mid 1890s, they were the first product of a new firm, probably struggling early in its existence with neighbors like Forgan and Morris to compete against and the firm was only in business for a short period, probably less than three years. With the vast majority of clubs available to collectors being from the D. & W. Auchterlonie period, Auchterlonie and Crosthwaite clubs also tend to be overshadowed.

Two primary name stamps exist. Which is the oldest, or first, is not known but with the firm in business such a short time it makes the relative ages of the two marks almost irrelevant.

The more unique of the two is the long rectangular box framing the firm's name. The lettering is very small and very simple. The long length of the stamp may have caused it to be abandoned early in its use since it would not adapt well to clubs with curved backs or other non-linear features.

Variety in advertising was not a consideration. This ad from The Golfer, *August 30, 1895 is similar to all the others.*

38

The more common mark has the firm name in two arcs creating a circle, with the word 'St Andrews' at the equator. It is much more compact than the first mark and as such could be used in more small areas and tight spaces. Variations of this mark include versions with and without the fern cleek mark used by Robert Condie. Two fern fronds are the most common, one fern or no ferns exist in lesser numbers.

An example of the scarce rectangular maker's mark used by Auchterlonie & Crosthwaite. This club is a gun metal putting cleek with flat back.

The cleek makers from whom Auchterlonie and Crosthwaite were able to purchase heads included the old guard of St Andrews: Robert Wilson, Willie Wilson and Robert White. James Anderson, down the road in Anstruther, was another available outlet, producing more iron heads than the aforementioned three St Andrews makers combined. However a majority of the heads seen today came from the Condie shop. Condie had only been in business himself a very short time, perhaps three or four years.

It is plausible that the even younger A. & C. firm was able to strike a deal with a hungry young cleek maker that benefited both houses. Tom Stewart was ostensibly setting

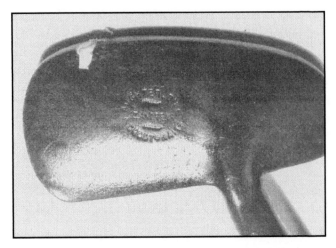

Of the very few Auchterlonie & Crosthwaite clubs that are held by collectors today, this centre shaft lofter is the most unusual. It was probably influenced by the crescent-shaped head of the Anderson Patent socketless iron a few years earlier, another centre shaft idea into which the golfing public never bought in. The mark is the usual round name mark with two fern fronds.

Unfortunately the quality of these photographs is not good; they were taken on the spot in an auction hall prior to the sale. The small white area near the toe of the club is a piece of tape.

40

This long blade lofting iron is typical of mid 1890s irons and typical of the sort Auchterlonie and Crosthwaite were selling. The circular mark has two of Robert Condie's fern fronds in the northern and southern hemispheres.

A standard steel blade-type putter, circa 1895, with the usual Auchterlonie and Crosthwaite mark including the two Condie fern fronds. Interestingly enough, the mark is upside down or diametrically opposite the same mark on other Auchterlonie and Crosthwaite clubs.

up his own shop in the year that Auchterlonie and Crosthwaite was established. Stewart's influence would be felt to a far greater degree at the next Auchterlonie firm.

Dissolution

In the middle of the year 1896 the trio dissolved their business relationship for unknown reasons. David and Willie went off and started the firm bearing both their names while Andrew Crosthwaite went into business with George Lorimer. Curiously, Crosthwaite & Lorimer retained the occupancy of the 146 North Street building while the Auchterlonies relocated a short distance away to 9 Albany Place. By 1899 Lorimer had left the partnership and Crosthwaite was the only name over the door.

My personal speculation is that the brothers left Andrew Crosthwaite of their own accord. The firm was founded as Auchterlonie and Crosthwaite by David Auchterlonie—the older of the two brothers and the more likely to strike out on his own—and Crosthwaite. Willie joined his brother shortly afterward. But since he was the Open Champion and garnered much of the attention, he probably wanted to be on equal footing with the two founders, that is, he wanted to be a full partner. Crosthwaite undoubtedly objected to the dilution of the profits so the two Auchterlonies left to establish their own firm and be equal partners. It is a theme that is so very plausible it would play out once more in the future.

A few years after that, Andrew Crosthwaite seems to have slipped into oblivion. George Lorimer continued doing what he did best: building high quality golf clubs while in the employ of others. His name resurfaced around 1905-1906 with a short-lived club making firm by the name of Wilson, Kirkaldy and Lorimer--sounding less like golfers and more like a consortium of solicitors. It was probably a partnership of convenience that lasted a year, at most. R.B. Wilson and Andra' Kirkaldy were two of St Andrews town's more irascible characters. Lorimer was tasked with making the clubs; Wilson did the marketing and Kirkaldy lent his name and competitive reputation.

Auchterlonie and Crosthwaite ad from The Golfer, *July 19, 1895. The fact that they had an agent in Glasgow meant their reputation had spread fairly quickly and opened a market in Scotland's largest city. It was a market that had far fewer club makers resident than St. Andrews. The golf retail business had not fully matured and it was not unusual for a retailer like Campbell, who was essentially a clothier, to handle golf clubs on the side.*

43

This turn of the century photo shows the Crosthwaite golf shop at 146 North Street, St Andrews, with Andrew Crosthwaite (center) and four of his club maker employees. The shop was the location where Crosthwaite and David Auchterlonie opened their golf shop in 1893, trading under the name of Auchterlonie & Crosthwaite, before parting company in 1896.

This ad was placed immediately prior to the brothers departing from their partnership with Andrew Crosthwaite. From Golfing, *April 15, 1896.*

44

The New Firm: D. & W. Auchterlonie

Assuming the two brothers dissolved their relationship with Andrew Crosthwaite in mid 1896 and removed themselves from the shop building that Crosthwaite retained, it most likely took them several months to get situated and ready for business. If they had decided early in the year to leave, they may have had a building already lined up. If not, they may have had to wait to get a piece of real estate for the business. This speculation is important because once they were back in business, they were in an enviable position, having taken the premises in Albany Place.

Albany Place is actually a continuation of North Street heading towards the golf courses. What made that location so ideal was that golfers walking to the links from the hotels in the center of town would probably pass through Albany Place. The new Auchterlonie shop would be one of the first they would encounter. Of course, the downside was that the Auchterlonies were commercial neighbors of D. Anderson & Sons (5 Ellice Place), Robert Forgan & Son and Tom Morris (both on The Links).

This location would serve as their commercial home from some time in 1896 until 1899 when they moved a few hundred yards west to 4 Pilmour Links and the shop that would be their business home until the doors closed following the passing of Willie Auchterlonie's son, Laurie, in 1987. Shortly afterward, it became a woolen goods shop. Presently, it remains a retail apparel outlet. A portion of the shop that was once D. & W. Auchterlonie now belongs to the "Auchterlonie's," Tom's former firm, and houses its antique clubs department.

45

Above: David (left end), Willie (right end) and their club makers posing with tools of the trade outside the old Albany Place shop sometime before 1899. Young Tom's head is visible in the doorway behind the apron-clad workers.

Below, Four staff members pose outside the door to the new D. & W. Auchterlonie shop at 4 Pilmour links. The door in the center of the building is 3 Pilmour Links, the access to the

apartment where David lived. The door on the far right leads to the rear entrances to both David's and Tom's apartments. The shop where Tom would move his business in 1934 (and live above) is located a few feet to the right of that door.

WILLIE AUCHTERLONIE¹ ST⁴ ANDREWS

The 1893 Open Champion Willie Auchterlonie, as he appeared in Golfing, *September 12, 1907.*

The masthead from an invoice dated 1906. The view of the shop is identical to the building in the photo on the opposite page with the added motorcar.

47

The Albany Place site was a small storefront, the bulk of the club making work being carried out in the old workshop behind 9 Union Street, at the other end of town. With success came the requirement for larger premises. This description of the move came from a 1901 *Golf Illustrated* article on the firm of D. & W. Auchterlonie.

> *The firm have just acquired a very valuable building site in Pilmour Links, where they propose to erect new premises, as their present shop in Albany Place is totally inadequate for their needs. It is in a most convenient situation, being on a direct road from the train station to the Links, and they hope to be able to open there soon.*

The new Pilmour Links location greatly expanded the firm's retail space and club repair facilities. Club manufacturing was still being performed at the shop at 9 Union Street. Lynne, a grand-daughter of James Auchterlonie, who lived in David Auchterlonie's house at 9 Union Street during the 1920s, recalled the activity that took place in the adjacent workshops. She remembered being told that the workshops were originally in the cellar under the house in Union Street. These had previously been used as a baker's and she remembers the old bread ovens, which would have been built into the walls, being used to store clubs. She was not sure, however, whether these would have been partially completed or finished clubs. The workshops then extended next door into the adjoining plumbers workshop.

That same *Golf Illustrated* article also provides some interesting metrics on the firm's relative business position. It states that the work rooms are under the personal supervision of Willie Auchterlonie. David was

MESSRS. D. AND W. AUCHTERLONIE'S NEW PREMISES

Above: This photograph was taken immediately after the D. & W. Auchterlonie firm moved from Albany Terrace to 4 Pilmour Links. The group on the doorstep include (L-R) Joe, Willie, Tom, George Lorimer, an indistinguishable figure, and David. In a few years the sign would be repainted to read "Golf Club Specialists" instead of "golf club and ball makers," as seen here.

Right: Club making brothers on the pavement in front of 4 Pilmour Links— Willie and David are wearing aprons; the identities of the two persons on the ends is unknown.

49

An advert from Golfing, January 7, 1904 showed sales agents in England and Ireland.

acknowledged as the timber expert, who evaluated each piece of lumber they purchased. Also, their staff had grown to sixteen workmen, which, for a club making firm, was significant. In the five years since they established the new firm, and eight years since they set up shop on their own, it seems they built a tidy business.

> *...and in St Andrews they command a very large proportion of the local trade. Indeed it has been said, and with a good deal of truth, that every third club you see in St Andrews is an Auchterlonie. They have also a very good connection all over the United Kingdom and abroad.*

If it was true they had around a third of the local trade, that was an astonishing percentage considering they were competing with Forgan and Morris—with Tom still alive and Robert Forgan having only just passed away. Forgan and Morris were St Andrews's favorite sons, whose businesses were well established, employing many local men, and we should assume they had, and were entitled

David Auchterlonie with staff and possibly his father, shown at the front door of the 4 Pilmour Links shop in May, 1914.

to, a bulk of the local business. But the Auchterlonie business was growing quickly, due in large part to riding the glory of Willie having won the Open. *Golf Illustrated* continued,

> *It has been said in these columns that, as a general rule, a club-maker who is a good player will make good clubs, and following this proposition further it will be concluded that the better player he is the better clubs will he make, and therefore if a Champion is got to make clubs, it is obvious he will turn out Champion articles. And so applying this principle to the case in point, it is little wonder that their clubs are in such favour."*

He was guilty of nothing new; Willie Park, the Champion Golfer of 1887 and 1889 had said the same thing a few years earlier.

51

The reason they may have garnered as much business as they did was their dedication to quality. It's difficult to imagine the Morris shop not producing as high a quality club as the Auchterlonie brothers but the latter certainly made quality hand production the cornerstone of their firm.

> *The Brothers Auchterlonie personally supervise all their work, and there is no doubt that this accounts, in a large degree, for the reputation they have gained for turning out only good, sound, well-wearing clubs. A shoddy article with "Auchterlonie" on it is indeed a rarity. Their wooden clubs are entirely hand-made from beginning to end, and their iron clubs hand forged. This fact is a recommendation in itself. In selecting the wood for their drivers and other wooden clubs the greatest care is taken, and every piece is subjected to a close scrutiny before it is allowed to pass into the hands of the workmen at all; no scruple being shown in rejecting any that do not come up to the scratch, more pieces often being rejected than passed. This process of examination is repeated at various stages in the transition of the rough wood into the finished club.*
> *Golf Illustrated, 1901*

It was the premise of producing top quality, hand made clubs that set them apart from the other firms, which were ramping up to more mechanized mass production methods in the early 20th century. David and Willie Auchterlonie had created a niche for themselves and would prosper in it.

The Stewart serpent mark was used on ladies and children's clubs. A club with this mark dates from around 1900.

The Registered Putting Cleek

If the Auchterlonie Special Registered Approaching Cleek was the club that helped put Auchterlonie & Crosthwaite on the map then another unique design would bring attention to D. & W. Auchterlonie as well. In April, 1903 they brought out the Auchterlonie Registered Putting Cleek. Perhaps the most interesting part of the club was the matching ball that was designed to go with the club.

The putting cleek had two dominant features. On the back it had a long, dome shaped ridge, running heel to toe, just a little above the centerline. This was intended to prevent the ball from jumping when initially struck by the face of the club. The other feature was a special face marking that can best be described as 'chain link.' Although putters with face scoring are not uncommon, the great majority of putters over time have not required any face markings. But Auchterlonies' did and this chain pattern matched the cover pattern of their new golf ball. Named the Auchterlonie Flyer, it was manufactured for the Auchterlonies by the Improved Golf Balls Company of Limehouse, London.

In 1903 rubber cored balls were taking the golf market by storm. Laurence Auchterlonie had not only won the US

53

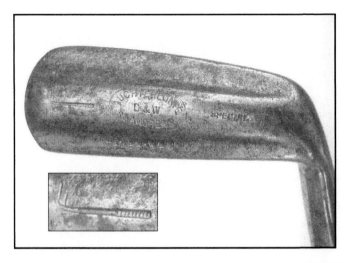

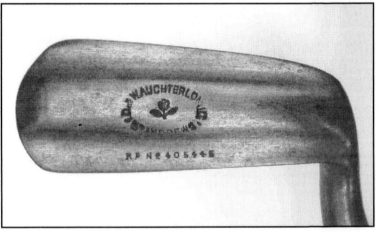

The Auchterlonie Registered Putting Cleek was available in a straight hosel or a wry neck variety. The club in the top photo bears the cleek mark—enlarged in the inset—of a small golf club, probably a mark the Auchterlonies used as their own. The registration number, 405445, appears on all clubs irrespective of the cleek maker.

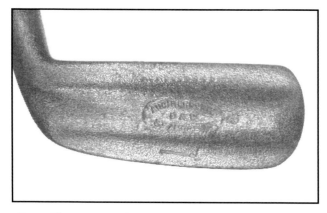

Top: The Registered Putting Cleek in the version made by Tom Stewart with the pipe mark below the name oval.

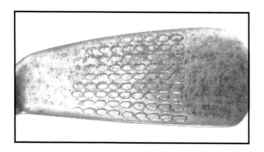

The "chain link" face pattern on the Registered Putting Cleek was part of the club's design; Stewart version (above) and Condie version (below).

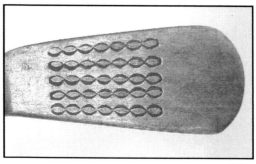

An Auchterlonie advertisement from The Golfers' Handbook, 1905 showing special billing for the Putting Cleek and the Approaching Cleek.

Open in 1902 but had done so by using the rubber cored ball. Now everyone had to play them and golf club makers, Auchterlonies included, made it a point to design clubs that were specially formulated to be compatible with and benefit from playing the new rubber center ball, like their own Auchterlonie Flyer.

Three different cleek makers producing the putting cleek for D. & W. Auchterlonie have been identified. The product introduction photo appearing in *Golfing*, May 7,

1903 shows the Registered Putting Cleek with Stewart's pipe cleek mark. Ostensibly, the Stewart club heads are the oldest. Similar club heads were obtained from Robert Condie's forge (with flower cleek mark). A very small number of these putting cleeks are found with the golf club cleek mark. Possibly used as a brand mark, I have only seen this mark on older Auchterlonie club heads. The source of the mark is uncertain but it is unlikely it was from Condie or Stewart.

Later versions of the Registered Putting Cleek kept the same form with the longitudinal weight on the back but the chain link face markings were dropped in favor of regular dot punching.

The Branch Location

In or about 1909, D. & W. Auchterlonie opened its first, and perhaps only, branch location in North Berwick. That

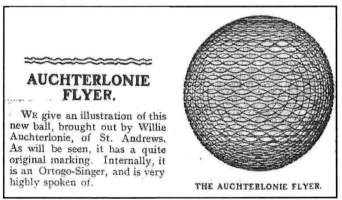

AUCHTERLONIE FLYER.

We give an illustration of this new ball, brought out by Willie Auchterlonie, of St. Andrews. As will be seen, it has a quite original marking. Internally, it is an Ortogo-Singer, and is very highly spoken of.

THE AUCHTERLONIE FLYER.

The Auchterlonie Flyer rubber cored golf ball had a cover pattern that matched the "chain link" markings on the club face. This announcement snippet is from Golf Illustrated, *1903.*

57

seaside resort town was similar to St Andrews in that it had very old golf links and was picturesquely oceanside. The move may have been a young firm gaining in popularity, flexing its marketing muscles but trying to invade someone else's turf. North Berwick already had a master club maker by the name of Bernard "Ben" Sayers who had started a ball and club making business in the early 1880s.

The North Berwick venture only lasted a few years for the Auchterlonie brothers. In 1910 Sayers's son, Ben, Jr., joined his father in North Berwick (after being a club professional elsewhere in Britain) and the old-style club making firm ramped up to more of a mass manufacturer. In 1914, the war began to sap the labor pool and most club making concerns went into a position of limited or zero production. D. & W. Auchterlonie clubs marked for North Berwick were produced between 1909 and 1915.

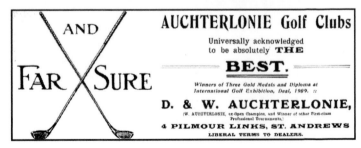

Auchterlonie ads from Golf *(top, 1899) and* Golfing *(1910).*

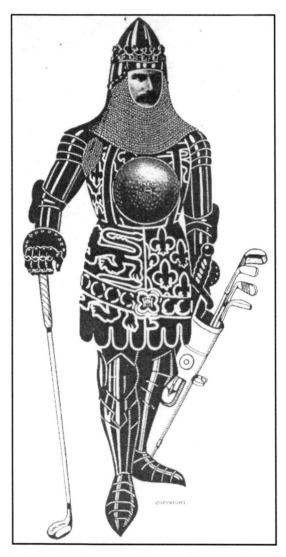

Willie Auchterlonie, in non-golf attire, from an ad promoting Spalding 'Black and White' brand golf balls, Golfing, *August 13, 1908. Fifteen years after his Open victory, he was still a marketable property.*

The Golf Clubs

The period of David and Willie Auchterlonie's club making activity lasted forty years. During that time they made a number of model series as well as turning out many clubs simply marked with the name of their firm. From the start, a majority of their iron clubs were forged by either Tom Stewart or Robert Condie and they were probably wise to stick with local St Andrews suppliers. Both Stewart and Condie were known for their quality and this undoubtedly enhanced the Auchterlonie reputation for quality as well.

It was the wooden clubs that carried out the quality image. Everything the Auchterlonies did, from selecting the best timber to using the finest finish on the wooden club heads, was geared to producing a top quality product for a discriminating clientele.

Willie Auchterlonie in his role as a club maker, from The Golf Trader, *1911.*

MR. WILLIE AUCHTERLONIE.

D. & W. Auchterlonie Early Clubs

Although it was made at the very end of the era of long headed woods, collectors would call this an Auchterlonie long nose club. This shape was produced by the D. & W. Auchterlonie firm from 1896 to around 1905. Putters of this shape were made into the 1920s and beyond.

This club is very similar to the one above it but it has lost its finish and is now lighter in color. The beech wood grain is clearly visible. At some point the face was shaved and given a hooked appearance; it is not original to the club.

61

D. & W. Auchterlonie Early Clubs

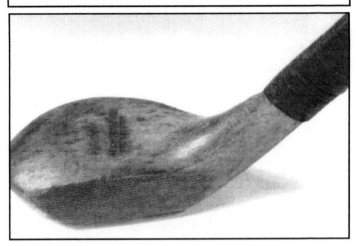

Top: A transitional, or semi-long nose, driver marked "Auchterlonie, The Champion." Dating from around 1900, the model name was evidence that Willie was still milking his championship honors.

Bottom: A very old Stewart-made blade putter with an encomium of markings: the older big-small double crescent mark, Stewart's pipe and personal inspection mark Circa 1900.

Ralph Livingston photo

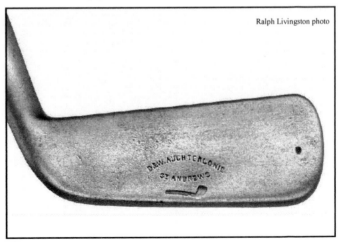

D. & W. Auchterlonie Early Clubs

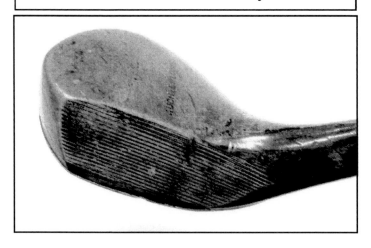

Top: *A splice head brassie with a slightly shorter, wider head than the transitional club pictured below. Circa 1905.*

Bottom: A splice head putter in a traditional shape from 1905-1910. It was the type that went out of fashion in the rest of Britain around 1905 but was continually made in St Andrews for many years afterward.

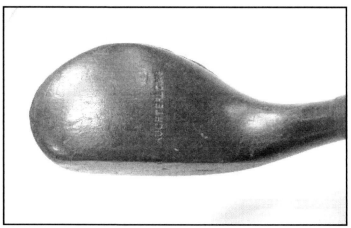

D. & W. Auchterlonie Approaching Cleek

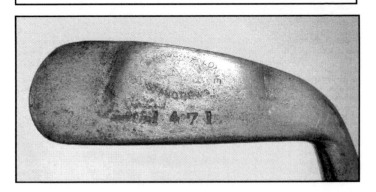

The Registered Approaching Cleek was designed by Willie Auchterlonie and first made while the brothers were part of Auchterlonie & Crosthwaite in 1896. They continued to make the club for another 25 years after they established D. & W. Auchterlonie. The well-worn example (top) carries no cleek mark to indicate who made the club head but has the registration number of 1471. The club below, slightly newer, is marked for Tom Stewart and has a registration number of 1662. With no trademark legend under the pipe, the club was made before 1904. With the low registration numbers, both clubs are most likely from before 1900.

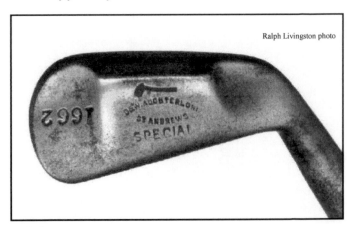

Ralph Livingston photo

D. & W. Auchterlonie Approaching Cleek

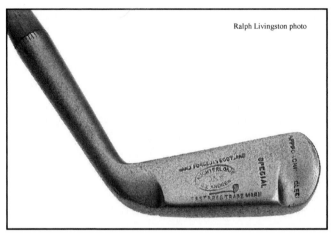

Ralph Livingston photo

Two later models of the Registered Approaching Cleek are shown with variant markings. The upper club has "Approaching Cleek" written down the toe, the lower club has it stamped along the top line. Both, circa 1910, no longer have registration numbers.

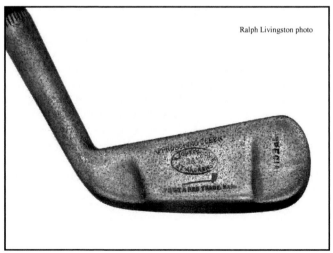

Ralph Livingston photo

Auchterlonie Iron Clubs...

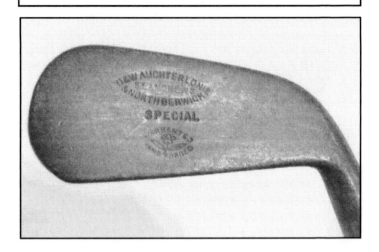

These two mid irons are very similar in both design and age. The main difference is that the bottom example has a flange sole for extra weight. Both have the Auchterlonie name oval with very pointed ends. In typical Condie fashion, the Condie flower cleek mark is located below the name oval. Circa 1910.

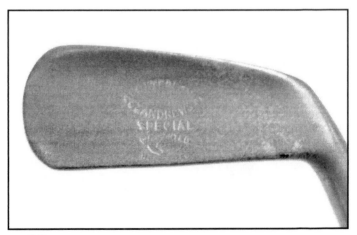

...From the forge of Robert Condie

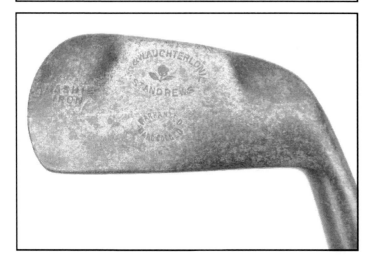

The 'musselback' style of the Registered Approaching Cleek was carried into other clubs. The mashie iron (above) has the same weighting pattern as the Approaching Cleek but it is deeper in the face, circa 1905. Ultimately the musselback shape was used in all types of irons including the mid iron pictured below.

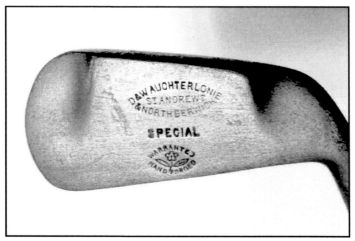

67

D. & W. Auchterlonie Clubs

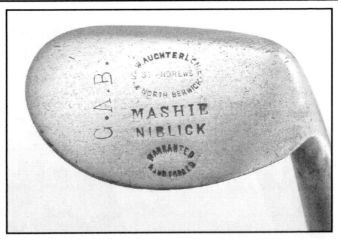

These two lofted irons are both smooth faced. The bottom club, a niblick sold by Thornton & Co., Ltd. of Edinburgh and Glasgow, is in a lady's weight and was probably forged by Robert Condie, circa 1905. The top club is in the recognizable flat soled "Foulis" mashie niblick shape and carries the Auchterlonie mark for St. Andrews and North Berwick. That mark was in use from 1909 to about 1915.

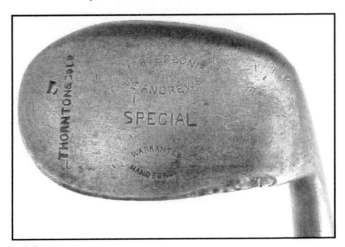

D. & W. Auchterlonie Clubs

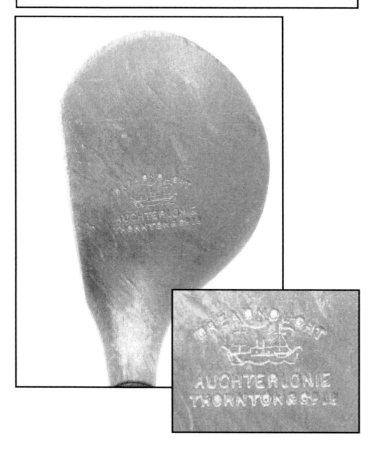

Ben Sayers invented the "dreadnought driver" for one of his customers, Admiral Jackie Fisher whose flagship was named H.M.S. Dreadnought, first of the 'all big-gun' battleships. It consisted of a slightly larger club head and a longer, whippier shaft. Other club makers capitalized on the design including the Auchterlonies. This club is unique among dreadnoughts with its warship maker's mark and was sold at Thornton's retail stores, circa 1920.

69

D. & W. Auchterlonie Clubs

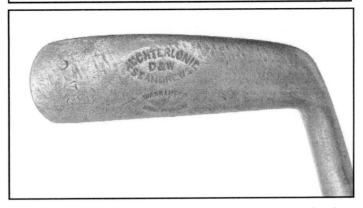

George Forrester invented the Gem model putter but within five years, every maker had his own copy on the market. This example dates from around 1910 and has an extra long blade.

John Wanamaker's department stores on the American east coast were major marketers of Scottish-made golf clubs,. This Auchterlonie socket driver carries Wanamaker's Taplow brand identifying mark. The Auchterlonie stamp is virtually the same as it was on the early long headed woods.

D. & W. Auchterlonie Clubs

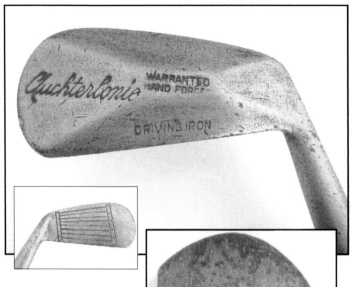

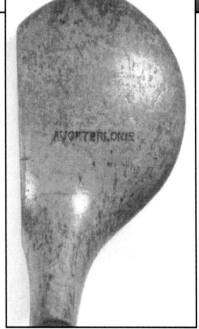

David and Willie produced this model line with their name in script about 1920. This driving iron is in the diamond back shape with a lined face.

Another socket head driver very simply marked "Auchterlonie." The finish has deteriorated a bit giving the club a freckled look.

71

D. & W. Auchterlonie Clubs

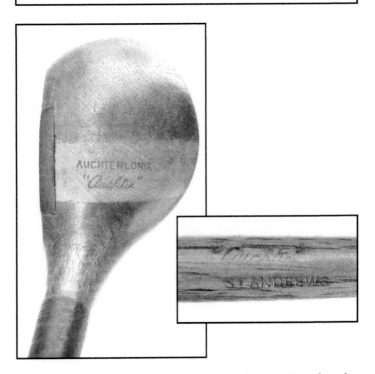

The "Auchtie" series of clubs was as close as David and Willie got to a named series. The stripe top driver was a popular finish in the 1920s. "Auchtie" clubs even had a shaft stamp that was a departure from the simple "Auchterlonie Selected" that had been used by the firm for decades.

A rustless mashie niblick from the same series.

D. & W. Auchterlonie Clubs

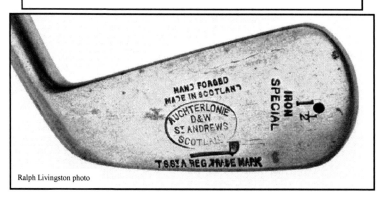

Ralph Livingston photo

A Tom Stewart-made 1-iron stamped for D. & W. Auchterlonie. The measurement on the club loft was probably altered to suit the owner, Robert T. Jones, Jr., and thus renumbered as 1 1/2.

During his march to the Grand Slam (the Impregnable Quadrilateral) of the 1930 season, Jones carried a mixed set of clubs originating from a wide assortment of club makers. His woods came from Jack White and George Duncan—two former Open Champions—while his irons originated in the shops of Stewart, James Donaldson, George Nicoll and Hendry & Bishop. His putter was a Spalding copy of his earlier possession, the legendary Calamity Jane, forged by Condie and assembled by William Winton. Each club was meticulously refined until it suited him perfectly.

This was the methodology by which golfers chose their equipment. If you picked up a club and the balance felt good, you gave it a try, no matter where the other clubs in you bag were from. In 1930, this practice was close to being forgotten. Manufacturers were producing more and more matched sets and hickory shaft clubs would be old technology in a few more years.

Jones was in St Andrews in 1926 for the Walker Cup. He had lost his golf clubs in a clubhouse fire in 1925 so perhaps it was on this trip that he visited the D. & W. Auchterlonie shop and purchased this club, rebuilding the selection of weapons from which he would assemble his finest playing set.

73

D. & W. Auchterlonie Clubs

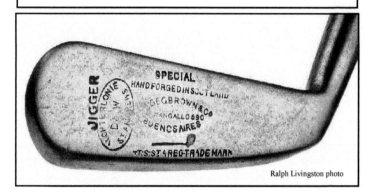

Ralph Livingston photo

Two irons exported to the Jorge G. Brown Company, Buenos Aires, Argentina. The upper club is a left handed jigger with the Brown mark more prominent than the Auchterlonie mark. The lower club is an iron with simpler markings. The inset photo is another Auchterlonie club exported to Lacey & Company, also in Buenos Aires. A 1909 article in Golfing stated that the Auchterlonies had dispatched three consignments of clubs to Argentina in the second half of the year.

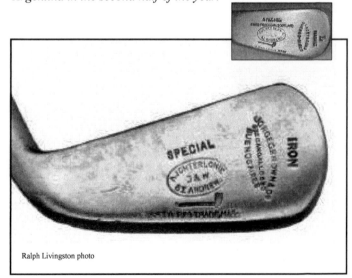

Ralph Livingston photo

D. & W. Auchterlonie Clubs

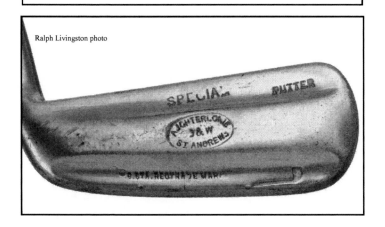

Ralph Livingston photo

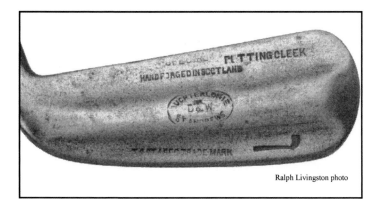

Ralph Livingston photo

Two more examples of the Auchterlonie Registered Putting Cleek except they no longer show the registration number. Both made by Tom Stewart the bottom club is still called a putting cleek while the top club, probably several years newer, is now just marked putter. The weight bar on the back of the top is thicker and weightier than the older bottom club.

75

D. & W. Auchterlonie Clubs

The *Auchterlonie Balance Putter* was patented in 1911.

The example at right shows the pattern of the markings and the patent number.

The three views of a different example, below, show a profile of the pointed toe.

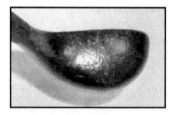

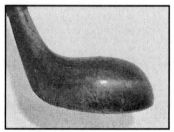

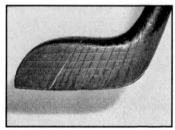

D. & W. Auchterlonie Clubs

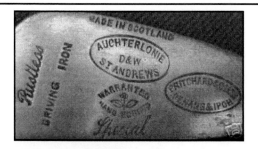

Top: A Condie-forged driving iron with common oval Auchterlonie name stamp. The club was exported to Penang, Malaysia.

Left: A typical Auchterlonie

Bottom: The boy's mashie is typical of the 1915 period. The name oval is still pointed and the rose remains below the maker's name. However the name of the club is stamped near the toe as is the small letter "B" which signifies it as a "boy's."

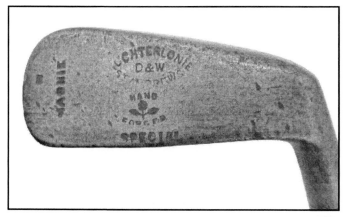

77

D. & W. Auchterlonie Clubs

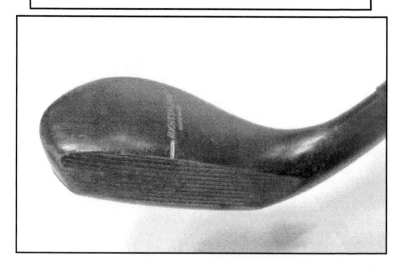

A wood putter of a type that was made from the 1930s into the 1970s, first by Willie Auchterlonie, then by his son Laurie. One of the 1970s vintage wood putters is shown below. T has the straight line name stamp identical to the late 19th century clubs on page 61 and the socket driver on page 71.

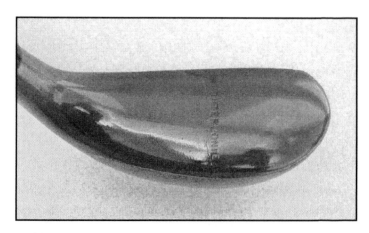

D. & W. Auchterlonie Miniature Clubs

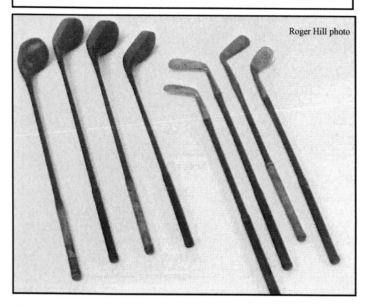

Roger Hill photo

This very attractive set of clubs, three woods, four irons and a wooden putter, were made by someone in the D. & W. Auchterlonie workshop, probably in the 1920s or 1930s. They are unusual because they are made to miniature scale, each club is about 10 inches long.

The woods are stamped "Auchterlonie, Hand Made," which is not atypical for Auchterlonie clubs. What makes it remarkable is that someone had a steel name stamp made with lettering so very small. The irons also have a similarly small name stamp befitting their small size. The rose cleek mark of Robert Condie is stamped on the irons.

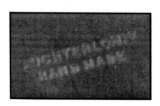

79

D. & W. Auchterlonie Minaiture Clubs

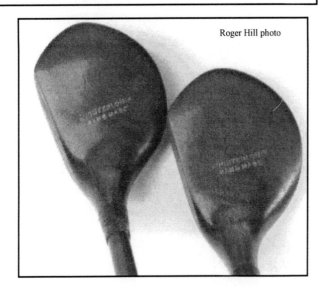

Roger Hill photo

Detailed views of the miniature clubs.

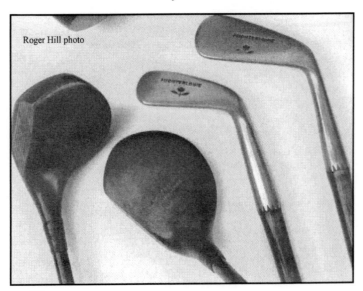

Roger Hill photo

Willie, the Honorary Professional

The Royal and Ancient Golf Club of St Andrews, golfdom's anchor at the first tee of the town's Old Course, does not employ a golf professional in the same sense as does the average country club. There is an Honorary Professional who assists and advises the club and its members. The first was Old Tom Morris, who gave the R and A many years service before retiring from the position in his old age in 1904. He was succeeded in 1910 by Andra' Kirkaldy who held the post until his death in 1934. The third honorary professional was Willie Auchterlonie who took the position in 1935.

With his playing career shifting from businessman to iconic retiree, Willie continued to be a very visible ambassador and statesman to the sport. He was present at all the normal Club functions, like the new R and A captain playing himself into the position, as well as those events of note that took place on the town links. Willie was also an honored guest at the Open Championship each year.

His son Laurie would be the fourth R and A Honorary Professional in 1965.

The Club Makers Exhibition

One of the milestone events in the history of the D. & W. Auchterlonie firm was the club makers' exhibition at the 1909 Open Championship at Deal. The club making business was in its heyday, possibly the most robust in

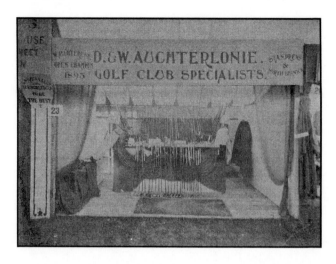

The first large scale club makers' exhibition held at an Open Championship took place at Deal in 1909. David and Willie Auchterlonie's firm took home a number of individual firsts as well as the Gold Medal for General Club Making. Their exhibit booth shown above may have been at the 1909 fair. The lower photo shows a later booth with banners touting their prize winning showing in 1909.

Thursday, June 17, 1909. The World of Golf.

TRIUMPHANT VICTORY

At the International Exhibition, Deal,
with Three Exhibits we secured

THREE FIRST PRIZES

AND

THREE GOLD MEDALS

ALSO

FIRST PRIZE

FOR

GENERAL CLUB MAKING.

For Incomparable Quality try our noted

HAND-MADE GOLF CLUBS.

They are used by all the leading players.

D. & W. AUCHTERLONIE,
(W. Auchterlonie, ex-open Champion, 1893),
Golf Club Specialists,
ST. ANDREWS.

316

David and Willie were quick to seize upon their prestigious awards at the 1909 Open Exhibition.

The top portion of an advertisement in The Golf Trader *(1911) shows D. & W. Auchterlonie displaying their club making gold medals from the 1909 Exhibition.*

A year after their recognition at the Deal Open Exhibition, David and Willie Auchterlonie took more honors at another club makers' exhibition in St. Andrews.

terms of sales and market growth. The purpose was straightforward: the club professionals congregated at the Open, so let them see the latest in golf equipment, course maintenance equipment and all golf related wares. A competition and trade show was organized in conjunction with the Open and dozens of firms involved with club making took part. It was, in essence, the inaugural forerunner to the giant PGA Merchandise Show staged annually in Orlando, Florida.

Judging was performed by three notables. Harold Hilton represented England, Robert Harris represented Scotland and Charles Gibson of Westward Ho! stood in for the Golf Professionals. David and Willie captured first place in the judging categories for Drivers and Brassies as well as first place in the General Club-Making Competition. Awards included gold medals and money. For several years afterward, they proudly made mention of their feats at the 1909 competition in their advertisements and promotional material.

The Business Fails

Inexplicably, the famous firm of D. & W. Auchterlonie declared bankruptcy in October, 1933. Their dedication to hand crafting high quality golf clubs didn't follow the trend to more mechanized methods once steel shafts were finally approved for use by the Royal and Ancient Golf Club in 1929.

Several factors probably contributed to their reversals in fortune. In the hearings held at the Sheriff's Court in Cupar, the reasons stated by the brothers for the loss of equity in the firm were the downturn in business for wood shafted clubs and the firm's liabilities from bad and questionable debts. The nature of those debts wasn't elaborated but it can be assumed that in the midst of the Great Depression, many retail firms that were selling Auchterlonie clubs may have found it difficult if not impossible to pay the manufacturer for the goods.

Willie gave testimony at that hearing but it was noted that David was too infirm to attend and that his deposition in regards to the matter was taken by the bailiff who also was empowered to administer the statutory oath. David died in 1934, shortly after the failure of the business.

Fifteen months after the bankruptcy court hearing, the 'stock in trade' of the firm was liquidated at public auction. The inventory, as it appeared in a notice in *The Scotsman*, was curious but also indicative of the root of the problem that caused the demise of the once prosperous firm. To be sold were 170 brassies and 60 drivers with wood shafts along with 82 hickory shafted clubs and 180 irons. Those numbers, when added, show that David and Willie had just under 500 wood shafted clubs. By contrast, the inventory only showed 60 steel shafted woods and 16 steel shafted irons. It may have been that they were caught with a large amount of old inventory but the more plausible explanation is that the brothers didn't see that the use of wood for golf club shafts was no longer accepted by the majority of the golfing public. Part of the inventory included cricket bats, hockey sticks and tennis racquets, all signs that the shop had stocked other lines in order to generate revenue.

At some point the business resumed under the same name in the same premises. However club making was no longer the mainstay. The shop in Pilmour Links became a retail establishment mostly catering to ready-made goods. To a great extent, it remained this way until the mid 1980s when Willie's son Laurie Auchterlonie passed away. Since the large majority of the old guard of St Andrews golfers and golf club makers—the Morrises, Forgans, Straths, Kirkaldys and Wilsons, Tom Stewart, Robert White--had all passed on, Willie Auchterlonie enjoyed the status of being the town's last resident Open Champion club maker. His responsibilities to the membership of the R and A probably kept his business afloat and he was able to preside for another two decades as the local hero.

He was always in the background, conspicuously though, at all R and A events and meetings as well as all the Opens that regularly returned to the Old Course. At the event of the Edinburgh and East Lothians PGA meeting in 1947 at the newly re-opened Longniddry course, Willie turned heads by partnering with Andrew Dowie in the foursomes competition, at a spry 75 years of age.

In September, 1937, *The Scotsman* reported that the D. & W. Auchterlonie in St Andrews shop was broken into and ransacked. Money was taken from a locked desk but more tragically Willie Auchterlonie's medals were stolen from a display case. Included were Willie's winner's medal from the 1893 Open Championship and six medals won by the firm in club making competitions.

One of Willie's most noteworthy tasks performed during his retirement was the redesign of the St Andrews Jubilee Golf Course in 1946, thirty-four years after its opening.

Willie's Son, Laurie Auchterlonie

In more modern times, the firm of D. & W. Auchterlonie

was run by Laurie, Willie's son and namesake of the uncle who was the American Open Champion. Born in 1904, Laurie was trained as a club maker, starting as an apprentice in his father's and uncle's shop after the end of the First World War. He continued to make clubs through the length of his career but his output was very small, working only when he felt like it. It was said that people would order hand made clubs from Laurie Auchterlonie and literally wait years for them to be finished.

Laurie began traveling to the United States, acting as a consultant in the area of golf history to many clubs and small museums. He sold 'collections' of antique clubs to several well-heeled clubs including the equipment that served as the nucleus for the display at the World Golf Hall of Fame at Pinehurst, North Carolina (now at World Golf Village, St. Augustine, Florida). Collections were also sold to Harbour Town on Hilton Head Island, South Carolina, Old Marsh, West Palm Beach, Florida and other country clubs. From about 1970 onward, Laurie probably spent more time traveling the world at the expense of his clients than he did running his business in St Andrews.

Like his father, Laurie served as the Honorary Professional to the R and A from 1965 to his death in 1987. Laurie and his wife, Bea, had no children and after their deaths, the shop was sold and used as retail space, ending ninety-one years of the D. & W. Auchterlonie firm.

He was also responsible for arranging the club display in the Royal and Ancient clubhouse in St Andrews. Several years after his demise, I was in the club room of the Royal & Ancient clubhouse viewing the antique golf clubs on the wall of their museum area with the club's historian, Bobby Burnet. I remarked to Bobby that I felt some of the dates assigned to the clubs on display were incorrect, a few by a considerable factor. Bobby replied, "Laurie wrote those descriptions. If he was within 400 yards, he considered it a direct hit."

One of the things I noticed, being a frequent visitor to St Andrews during my time at the University of Dundee in the early 1970s, was that Laurie's shop, the D. & W. Auchterlonie shop, was rarely open for business. When I peered in the windows, the place was haphazardly arranged with a very antiquarian air to it, in no way resembling a modern retail business. It stood quietly, as if it was a relic of the past, a monument to the glory days of St Andrews golfers.

Twice I was able to venture into the shop for a few minutes and meet Laurie. On the surface he was gruff, officious and distant but one time when I asked him a question of historical significance, he opened up, conversed freely with considerable animation and displayed the soul of an old St Andrean—one who had lived the game among the greats in the Auld Grey Toun.

Dr. Gary Wiren, the golf instructor, coach, author and historian, had an early relationship with Laurie Auchterlonie, starting in the 1960s. Gary had run an advert in *The Scotsman* seeking antique clubs and Laurie had responded. Gary was living in Oregon at the time and invited Laurie to come to the Pacific Northwest for a speaking tour.

In 1972 Gary moved to Florida to work at the PGA of America and convinced his employers to purchase antique clubs from Laurie to start a small collection. This would become the nucleus for the World Golf Hall of Fame Museum at Pinehurst, North Carolina. The museum was housed in a one-story brick building just beyond the green

on the fourth hole of the famous Number 2 golf course. In the early 1990s, that collection, including the Auchterlonie clubs, was moved to St. Augustine, Florida to be part of the new museum at World Golf Village.

This fairly standard blade putter, forged by Stewart, was made in the 1930s. The shaft is marked for Laurie Auchterlonie, who may have assembled it or re-shafted the head after inheriting the shop from his father, Willie, in the early 1960s.

As a club maker, Laurie held a lofty reputation. His work was exceptionally fine; he just did not make many clubs in his later years. He made a putter for President Eisenhower in 1956 and also a replica 18th century play club for Arnold Palmer to use on the occasion of driving himself in as Captain of the South Carolina Golf Club, Hilton Head Island, South Carolina.

Laurie Auchterlonie

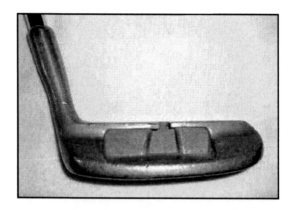

Laurie Auchterlonie became well known throughout golf circles in Britain from his Sunday Post putters. Any golfer who recorded a hole in one in a medal competition was awarded one of these Laurie Auchterlonie putters by the newspaper.

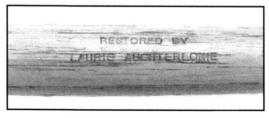

Clubs restored by Laurie Auchterlonie can be found in museums and private collections. Most carry this shaft stamp identifying the club as having been restored by Laurie.

91

The PGA of America bought a large number of antique clubs and artifacts from Laurie in the 1970s. This group of clubs became the nucleus for the displays at the World Golf Hall of Fame at Pinehurst, North Carolina. The Hall of Fame Museum opened in 1974 and closed in 1993 when the decision was made to incorporate the museum's holdings at the new museum complex at World Golf Village in St. Augustine, Florida.

Some of Laurie's finest work went into his wood head clubs. His persimmon woods never were fitted with face inserts, "the ball wasn't meant to hit a bit of plastic," he said. The bottom woods were stamped with his name, the driver on the left has a decal name.

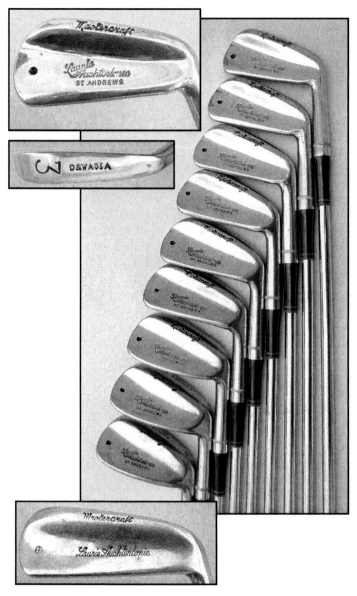

Mastercraft Brand irons and putter (bottom) from the shop of D. & W. Auchterlonie, made by Laurie.

93

Laurence Auchterlonie, Champion

Willie Auchterlonie may have been the most visible of the brothers with his Open Championship and, later his position serving the Royal and Ancient Golf Club, but day in and day out, brother Laurence may have been the best and most consistent golfer in the family.

Coming into the world in 1867, he was younger than James, Joseph and David but was born before Willie and Tom. Laurie was an active member of the St Andrews Golf Club, joining in 1888 and frequently playing in their competitions. His early accomplishments included carrying off the club's aggregate medal for the year's play, and in 1891 he won the gold medal presented to the local clubs by the Royal and Ancient, a medal he would win six more times. Laurie also partnered with British Amateur Champion Mr. P.C. Anderson to win the *Times* Trophy in 1894. His greatest accomplishment while playing in his homeland was to win the Scottish Amateur Championship in 1897, after having finished second each of the two prior years.

Laurie played as an amateur in the 1895 Open

Laurie Auchterlonie,
The Golfer, *8-18-1897*

MR. LAURENCE AUCHTERLONIE.

Championship at St Andrews finishing in a remarkable tie for 13th place (with Mr. J. Robb), 18 strokes behind J.H. Taylor. His brother Willie finished in a disappointing 31st place, just two years after w i n n i n g t h e championship.

Laurie Takes the American Plunge

Ironically, despite having a family name rapidly on the ascent in golf making circles in St Andrews with certain recognition, he chose to leave Fife and head to America.

> *Mr. Lawrence Auchterlonie, brother of Willie, the professional, sailed last week for a golfing tour in the United States. He was accompanied by Fred Herd, the Open champion of America, and by two other St Andrews golfers.*
>
> *Golf (U.K.) March 17, 1899*

The other St Andrews lads that traveled with Auchterlonie and Herd on the ship "Lucania" were William Leslie and William Yeoman. Not mentioned was a fifth member of

LAWRENCE AUCHTERLONIE.
Western Open Champion.

Laurie Auchterlonie following his Western Open victory, October, 1901

the star-studded traveling party, Carnoustie's Willie Smith. In that crew were three current or future US Open Champions. Yeoman would be a noted club manufacturer in Chicago and Leslie a well-known club pro around Chicago. He began working at Glen View as Auchterlonie's assistant and when Laurie moved on, Leslie was made the professional. Bill Yeoman worked with Smith and Herd at Washington Park for one year (as Smith, Herd and Yeoman) before settling in with Herd in a more longstanding firm, Herd & Yeoman.

Laurie's ultimate destination was Chicago but when the boat docked in New York, he was not allowed to disembark. New York labor leaders thought he was under contract with the Glen View club in Chicago's northern suburbs and using foreign labor under contract was, at the time, illegal.

> *The labour leaders of Chicago threaten to oppose the coming of Auchterlonie to this country, under the ground that his engagement by a well-known club lies within the provisions of the contract labour law. Up to this time the question has not*

been raised, but the provision could certainly be enforced if the fact of the contract can be proved. The "pro" who thinks of coming over should be careful, or he may not be allowed to land.

(Contributed by W.G. Van Tassel Sutphen,
the American golfer and writer)
Golf (*U.K.*) *March 24, 1899*

The situation was soon resolved and possibly there is a clue in the first notice—that Laurie was going on a tour of America. Had he already entered into a contract he might have been reported to be heading to the Glen View Club. At any rate, he began life as a club professional to a fairly affluent American club in 1899. We have to assume that he was welcomed to the Chicago area by Jim Foulis, Jr. at Chicago Golf, who was not only a St Andrean but a former fellow member of the St Andrews Golf Club.

The 1902 U.S. Open Championship

During his first summer in the States, Laurie brought immediate media attention to himself by coming in second to Willie Smith in the first Western Open conducted by the Western Golf Association. There was no Western Open championship in 1900 but two open tournaments brought together the best golfers to tune up prior to the Open. Chicago's Belmont club hosted the pros who had gathered for a shot at beating Harry Vardon. However, Vardon cancelled at the last minute. Davie Bell won but Laurie Auchterlonie was only a stroke behind. A week later, at Oconomowoc, Wisconsin, Laurie whipped a classy field as he bested Alex Smith and Willie Anderson (T-2) and Willie Smith and Davie Bell (T-4).

> *Auchterlonie's showing certainly makes him a dangerous candidate in the coming championship, though it is doubtful if he can hold his own with Champion [Willie] Smith at the long game.*
>
> *Golf (US), 1900*

In 1901, playing at Midlothian, in Chicago's south

A Triumph for St. Andrews.

Laurence Auchterlonie,
Open Champion of America.

[See page 8.

This tribute photo of Laurie Auchterlonie, Golf Champion of America, was run in (British) Golfing, *October 30, 1902*

suburbs, Laurie was victorious in the Western Open. He had made a name for himself, although those were times when there was a great divide between the more dominant "eastern" golfers and those "western" golfers, mainly from the Chicago area. Midwestern golfers knew him well but there was still an East Coast bias.

LAURENCE AUCHTERLONIE.

Laurie Auchterlonie, as seen in (U.S.) Golf, November, 1902

The next year, 1902, he would win the big one. In the run up to the National Open, Laurie showed he was gathering momentum when he won a professional tournament at the Western Ho! club, west of Chicago. Laurie won handily beating Davie Bell, his closest competitor, by three strokes, 152-155. A snapshot of the state of golf in America at that time reflects the preponderance of Scotsmen in the golf business. The first fourteen places in the Westward Ho! tournament were all won by golfers from East Scotland—Carnoustie, St Andrews and the Edinburgh-Lothians area.

The 1902 US Open was contested at the Garden City Golf Club on Long Island, Walter Travis's home course and one that he had, himself, laid out. Laurie finished the first round in second place, one stroke off the pace but was the leader after rounds two, three and four. His four rounds in the 70s (78, 78, 74, 77=307) constituted the first time any player had scored in the 70s in each round and his steady play placed him six strokes ahead of Stewart Gardner and amateur Walter Travis, tied at 313. The 1902 Open will be remembered as the first US championship where the new Haskell rubber core ball was used. As a result, scores were significantly lower than past years. The impact the rubber core ball can be seen in the performance of future Open champion Alex Smith. He shot a 331 to finish in 18th place in 1902. A year earlier, he carded the same score to get into a playoff with Willie Anderson (eventually losing the championship by a stroke).

Laurie's victory contributed to a clean sweep for Glen View. As the club professional, he tutored Mr. Louis James, the 1902 Amateur Champion and Miss Anthony, the Ladies Open Champion.

Laurie Auchterlonie's record in US Open competition:

1899	Baltimore CC	T-9
1900	Chicago Golf	4th
1901	Myopia Hunt	T-5
1902	Garden City	1st
1903	Baltusrol	7th
1904	Glen View	T-4
1905	Myopia Hunt	24th
1906	Onwentsia	T-3
1907	Philadelphia Cricket	T-11
1908	Myopia Hunt	T-21
1909	Englewood	T-23

In his first six US Opens he had six top 10 finishes.

In those early days of golf, the notion of 'major'

tournaments had not been promoted by the media but the US Open and the Western Open were bigger than any other tournaments in North America. For many years, the Western Golf Association, which conducted the Western Open and Western Amateur, rivaled the United States Golf Association in importance and influence. At a time when transportation and communication separated the east coast from the Midwest, the WGA served Midwestern clubs as well as those west of the Mississippi with guidance on rules, competitions and membership services. Laurie had accomplished a considerable feat winning the two 'majors' in consecutive years.

As a professional in America, Laurie was able to work in an environment which the Scots could never have dreamt of. American clubs supported professional golfers with comparatively large salaries, fringe benefits and local visibility. Like many of his counterparts, he was able to

An ad promoting Florida winter golf showing Laurie at Belleair in the winter of 1901 from (U.S.) Golf, 1901.

101

secure a winter position in a warm weather clime—Florida—when the courses in Chicago were frozen and snowbound.

John D. Dunn and the Western Golf Association made arrangements for golf play at five Florida hotels, which served as early warm weather resorts. Tournaments were held as a way to generate interest in the sport that was growing by leaps and bounds. Laurie was attached to the course at the Hotel Belleview in Belleair, near Clearwater, in the winters of 1901 and 1902.

Laurie's Return to St Andrews

Laurie returned to St Andrews from Chicago in 1911 and remained in Scotland for the remainder of his life. With his brother Joe, who was five years his elder, he was a constant figure on the links. Only after Joe became too infirm to continue playing did Laurie also hang up his clubs.

In 1935, at the age of 67, Laurie equaled the professional record of the Old Course set up by George Duncan, with a round of 68. He equaled the score under championship conditions, while playing in the August monthly medal competition. During his tenure as a member of the St Andrews Golf Club he won every competition and prize offered by the club, which made him an honorary member in 1938.

Laurence Auchterlonie, the former Champion of America, died in St Andrews in 1948 at the age of 80. He was survived by his wife Christina and two children, a son,

James, and daughter, Chrissie, both school teachers.

Laurie Auchterlonie's Club

To date, I have seen only one club with Laurie's name stamp, his own model putter called the "Professional." During his tenure as professional at Glen View, he most likely imported clubs made by his brothers' firm in St Andrews, stamped with the D. & W. Auchterlonie name.

Above: Laurie Auchterlonie's "Professional" model putter, made during his days at the Glen View Golf Club, north of Chicago. On the bottom edge of the weight flange, between the oval mark and the word "Professional," the serial number (190) and the date, 1907, are stamped. The shaft stamp is simply "Auchterlonie" in brackets.

Left: A profile of the club from the toe end shows the shape of the back weight.

103

Joseph Auchterlonie, Club Maker

While David, Willie and Laurie were accorded all the fame, their brother Joseph stayed in the workroom, so to speak, working as a club maker. When the shop was at its height of manufacturing capacity, Joe probably served as a foreman. Besides showing up in a few group photographs and the Town Directory, Joe kept a much lower profile than his brothers, the proprietors of the business.

Oddly enough, despite being in the club making background most of his life, he was accorded a report in a golf periodical of his forthcoming wedding.

> *The workmen in the employment of Messrs. D. & W. Auchterlonie had a very enjoyable smoker at the Cross Keys Hotel last week. The occasion was the presentation of a wedding gift to Mr. Joseph Auchterlonie. Mr. James Stevens presided, and handed over the gift, in the name of the subscribers wished Mr. Auchterlonie and his prospective partner all happiness and prosperity in their married life.*
>
> *Golfing, December 16, 1909*

At the time of this pre-nuptial party, he was 46 years old. Having worked as a plasterer first, he eventually came to work as a club maker, at age 30, for his brothers around the time they opened their own business at Ellice Place. This was his second marriage; with his first wife he had raised three sons.

Joe was a highly skilled golfer and the St Andrews Golf Club group photograph on page 26 shows him with two of the club's competition medals hanging around his neck.

He passed away in 1948, slightly after his younger brother and golf partner, Laurie.

Joe's three sons all became golf professionals, though away from Britain. Eldest son David went to the resort at Carlsbad, then in Austria, now the Czech Republic, from 1912-1919, later moving to Potchefstroom, South Africa.

Second son Henry, better known as Harry (born 1890), came to America in 1915 heading for Chicago. However, he never got farther than Arcola, New Jersey, where he became the Arcola Golf Club's professional. He was there for one year before moving to New York. In a freak accident he was electrocuted five years later when he was moving a downed high voltage wire at his post at the Sherwood Forest Club, near Annapolis, Maryland where he had been for two years.

> *Auchterlonie met his death while trying to free his wife and young nephew, Daniel McCracken, who had become entangled in the wire. The accident happened outside his own cottage. He had succeeded in pulling the wire from them, and in stepping back his foot came in contact with an iron water pipe. The full charge of the current passed through his body and he fell dead..*
>
> *New York Times, July 10, 1922*

The youngest son, Joseph, Jr. (born 1893), came to America in 1919. He secured a position at Westchester Country Club outside New York City.

Auchterlonies in Golf Course Design

The initial reputation of the Auchterlonie family was one of brilliant players of golf but as their businesses matured, they were better known as makers of high quality golf implements. The third side to that triangle of skills was course layout. Few references chronicle their work in design but several examples exist. Being well known in golfing circles, they were undoubtedly called upon to lend their expertise in the layout of courses, not often it seems, but called upon all the same.

The available information is confusing. Willie and Laurie laid out the course at the Milngavie Golf Club, north of Glasgow. The Royal & Ancient handbook says "the Auchterlonies" also worked the Ranfurly Castle Golf Club in 1889*, the Campsie G.C. course in 1897 and the St. Fillans G.C. course in 1903. With Laurie in America in 1903, if work was done at St. Fillan's, it would have been Willie with either David, or Tom, or both. The Lamash G.C.* is also on the R. & A. list as being their work.

When they hired the Auchterlonies, Milngavie not only got a hot property, the Open Champion of a year earlier, but they got a good financial deal, too.

In the space of the intervening eight days [from

*Ranfurly Castle G.C. at Bridge of Weir was founded in 1888 but reconstituted as a club company in 1904. Willie Auchterlonie and Andra' Kirkaldy performed the work on the course around this later date, according to the Ranfurly Castle club history. Lamash, on Arran, was also founded as a club in 1890, earlier than would suggest Auchterlonie involvement at that time. Their work might well have been later on.

106

the time the club agreed to begin work on a course] the ground had been surveyed and, with the help of the brothers Auchterlonie from St Andrews, a group of ten enthusiasts had staked out nine holes. The Auchterlonies said "it was one of the best inland courses they knew of but the ground was not large enough for an 18 hole course." The cost of their advice was a fee of one guinea, plus railway fare and tea—definitely a sound investment. *

That layout work took place in 1895. On April 11, 1896 the Auchterlonies were back at Milngavie to play an exhibition match on the newly constructed course. Laurie and Willie ended the 36 hole affair deadlocked at 162 with Laurie having shot the low 9 (36) and 18 (75). The club paid the brothers £4 for the exhibition plus 3 shillings 8 pence for lunches.

Laurie, during the winters in Florida, was said to have laid out the first course that had turf in that state. Many of the southern courses were first played with sand greens and natural-state fairways that resembled 'waste areas' on modern designs.

A project that also bears Laurie Auchterlonie's handprint may also be one of the most unusual in golf architecture. The project is known as The Kameruka Estate, located in southern New South Wales, Australia. The Estate was a resort-type getaway that included a luxury hotel and a nine hole golf course. The course was designed by Laurie who never actually set foot in Australia. The work was done through the mail using topographic maps with the

* From *Milngavie Golf Club, 1895-1995, The First Hundred Years* by Robert M. Sim.

107

construction work overseen by Sir Robert Lucas Lucas-Tooth.

Late in his career, after World War II, Willie Auchterlonie supervised the lengthening of St Andrews' Jubilee Course.

Willie Auchterlonie, circa 1935, possibly a photo taken around the time he was appointed as the Honorary Professional to the Royal and Ancient Golf Club.

Willie Auchterlonie and his brother Laurie, in their twilight years, standing on the steps of the shop. Although they are holding wood shaft clubs this photo probably dates from the 1940s.

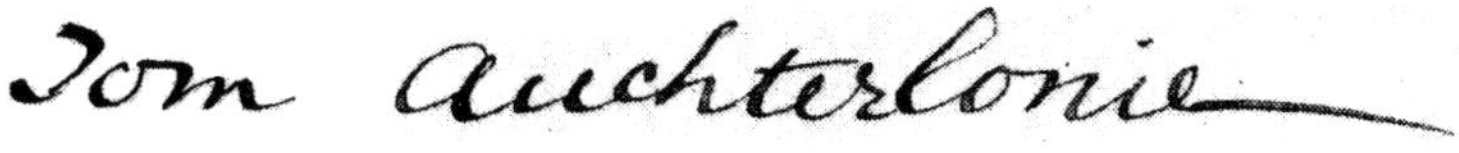

Wm Auchterlonie

Laurie Auchterlonie

Tom Auchterlonie

*A young, very dapper Tom Auchterlonie on the doorstep to the
D. & W. Auchterlonie shop at Albany Place with an unidentified
club maker by his side.   This photo had to have been taken
between 1896, the year Tom went to work for David and Willie,
and 1899, the year the firm moved to Pilmour Links.   The clubs
displayed in the window all have paper wrappers protecting the
calfskin grips, the way new clubs were shipped.*

110

Tom Auchterlonie

The youngest of the six sons, the proverbial baby of the family, Tom Auchterlonie was probably the most successful in the end. When he was born in 1879, David was already 14 or 15, Laurie was 11 and Willie was 6 so he was almost a generation apart from his elder siblings.

As a young lad, Tom had an accident, falling off a pile of lobster traps in the harbor area. His knee cap was shattered and required serious surgery. The result was that for the remainder of his life one leg was slightly shorter than the other and he had special boots to compensate. This situation apparently didn't affect him much as he was able to play scratch golf as a young man and throughout much of his life.

The Magic Club

"Hi, sonny, here's a club for ye," said David Blythe (of club makers Anderson & Blythe fame). Tom Auchterlonie was the young boy and Blythe tossed him the head of an old lofting iron that he was ready to place into the trash. He cleaned it up and his brother put in a new shaft. That occurred around 1888.

Tom said that as a lad he would go to the course with that same 'old faithful' club and a pocket full of balls. From the area around Forgan's shop (close to the 18th green on the Old Course) he would hit balls over the wall and onto the last green of the Old Course. He never went far from the pin and during one of these practice sessions Old Tom spotted him and made him an offer for the club. Saying that it was a present, wee Tom Auchterlonie refused to part with it. Admiringly, Old Tom told him, "You're a great wee laddie. Good luck to you. And may you always hae such good principles."

Later, he would practice negotiating stymies with that club. On one occasion, he popped twenty-four consecutive stymies with his 'miracle club.' An older man, witnessing this, bet him he couldn't do another eight. Tom did and won a handsome sum of money. That club remained in his bag well into his adult years.

Tom recalled some of his early instruction in golf, when he finally graduated to playing with proper clubs and balls on the Old Course, was from Tom Morris himself, who would shout instructions from his house window (which overlooked the fairway and green of the eighteenth hole).

As a five-year-old youngster, Tom took an interest in club making by watching Geordie Lorimer and Bob Martin making clubs in the Tom Morris workshop. When he was a schoolboy, he began making experimental club heads from spoiled blocks of wood he found in David & Willie's workshop. He would soon be working for them full time.

Tom and his wife Isabella (usually known as Bella) had two sons, Norman and Eric. Both were educated in St

Above: Thomas and Isabella Auchterlonie, possibly as an engaged couple or newly married, after the turn of the century.

Left: parents Bella and Tom with Norman and Eric. Eric was born in 1911 so this photo might have been taken around 1914 or 1915.

113

Andrews with Norman becoming a medical doctor. Tom assisted Norman financially to secure a practice in Invergordon, northern Scotland with the understanding that Eric would succeed him in the club making business.

Away from the shop and the links, Tom had two domestic avocations. For a while he bred and raised Scottish Terriers, having the ubiquitous black Scottie and white West Highland terrier around the house as pets. Later on, he was a canary and small bird breeder, judging avian competitions as well and specializing in the breeding of Scotch Fancy Canaries. Starting in 1927 he won the Scotch Fancy Cup three times at Dundee, at Edinburgh and at leading shows in Britain. He was responsible for the aviary set up in Kinburn Park in St Andrews.

Tom passed away in 1962 at the age of 83 running a highly successful business until the end. Active in St Andrews civic affairs, he was a popular and respected citizen of the town.

The New Business: Tom Breaks Away

For over 65 years St Andrews supported two Auchterlonie golf shops. For nearly a half century, the two shops occupied premises virtually one door apart on Pilmour Links. Certainly some visitors to the town must have wondered how there came to be two similar golf businesses. The similarity in the Auchterlonie name suggested it was more than a coincidence.

Tom Auchterlonie, then seventeen years old, went to work for his older brothers David and Willie in their shop when it was located in Albany Place, in 1896. Whether or not he was apprenticed to them is unclear but starting at that age

Two photos of Tom Auchterlonie from the same sitting, probably taken between 1900 and 1905.

he must have been. However, he worked for them through his apprenticeship and as a full employee for a solid twenty-three years. As he learned the trade he became very proficient at both the business and the club making activities. In time he successfully managed the business for his brothers, undoubtedly spending more time there than they did.

Tom Auchterlonie may never have reached his full potential as a club maker if his designs on leaving St Andrews come to fruition. In 1904 he applied for a position as the head professional to the West Lancashire Ladies' Golf Club in Blundellsands. At the time he applied for the position, he was 25 years old and had probably finished his apprenticeship and was working for his brothers as a full employee. Although not much has been written about his abilities on the links, Tom was a scratch golfer as a young man.

One of several candidates for the post, Tom was told by the secretary the club could not guarantee him £2 per week, only 30/- (shillings) with the added income of 2/- per hour lesson of which he was allowed to give two lessons per day. After 5:00 PM he was off the clock at the club and could dispense additional lessons. Being the brother of an Open Champion had sway but apparently not enough sway. Tom failed to get the job and continued working for his brothers for another fifteen years.

At some point, Tom suggested that he had paid his dues and his reward should be forthcoming—a full partnership. He was good at the business, he had been an employee for twenty-three years, he was family and he also had a family of his own to support. For whatever reasons, David and Willie refused to cut him in, just as Andrew Crosthwaite had probably refused to take Willie into the partnership.

The sublimely confident Tom Auchterlonie made a most risky decision and chose to leave his own brothers. In 1919, with the World War over and the golf business reviving, Tom went into business for himself doing what he best knew, making high quality golf clubs.

The Ellice Place Shop

The first premises Tom occupied was at 2 Ellice Place, which is an extension of North Street near the Links. He had probably sunken his life savings into the concern. The townspeople, accustomed to the D. & W. Auchterlonie shop as well as the dozen other club shops in St Andrews, viewed his potential success with some skepticism.

Tom's early iron club heads were procured from both Robert Condie and Tom Stewart and it can be assumed he had no trouble getting trade credit from them based on the fine record he amassed while working for his brothers. If Tom had kept David and Willie successful, then he had most assuredly mastered the art of producing and marketing top-quality hand made golf clubs. If there was any town in the world where the art of making superior golf clubs was appreciated, it was St Andrews. This item, from *The Sports Trader* eight years before Tom departed from D. & W. Auchterlonie, hints of his superior business acumen.

> *"Tom Auchterlonie, who acts as manager, is the youngest of the quartette and a smart business man. Up to date in his ideas and a real golf expert, much of the administrative work is entirely left to him and the selling side is all in his hands."*

> *The Sports Trader, August 1911*

117

This view of Tom Auchterlonie's Ellice Place shop is taken from a 1925 newspaper clipping. He occupied these premises from 1919 to 1934.

Eric, Tom's younger son, went to work for his father as an apprentice club maker at age 17 in 1928, while the business was still situated at Ellice Place.

The Schism

When Tom Auchterlonie decided to leave his brothers' business and begin his own club making firm, it was more than a simple familial parting of the ways. His departure caused a fracture in the family structure that was never repaired. It is impossible to say what the precise cause of the acrimony may have been but it was deep, painful and very final. In his professional life, Tom showed that he was a man of conviction and high moral principles. When his brothers failed to include him in the family firm as a full partner he was undoubtedly wounded.

There are only bits and pieces remaining of the feud that can stand analysis eighty-five years later. Two advertisements, one for each firm, run in the years following 1919, try to show exclusivity. Tom's ad intimates that his shop is not related to any other by stating "Only Address—." David and Willie's ad proclaims "THE ORIGINAL FIRM, And no connection to any other firm of the same name." Clearly they did not want to acknowledge the other's presence. The situation became worse, not better, when Tom moved to a new store at Golf Place/Pilmour Links, only a door away from the D. & W. shop.

> *"By the way, we are asked by Mr. Tom Auchterlonie to say that there is no truth to the reports that have been circulated to the effect that he has had the misfortune to go into liquidation. Notices of sequestration regarding a St Andrews firm of the same name that appear from time to time do not apply to him."*
> *The Sports Trader, April 1934*

Tom was obviously trying to differentiate himself from news of the financial troubles embroiling the business of his two older brothers while *The Scotsman* ran headlines like this:

GOLF CLUB FIRM FAILS

Steel Clubs and Bad Debts

From 1919 onward, it appears that the two sides of the family were not on speaking terms. This complete

119

avoidance continued into the next generation when Laurie ran the D. & W. shop and Eric was in charge of Tom's business.

A noteworthy instance of the chasm that separated the two firms was seen in 1934 when Tom offered to buy the rights to the D. & W. Auchterlonie trade name after that firm was declared insolvent. This move showed the hard-nosed business acumen that made him successful. He wrote the solicitors, Henderson & Logie, handling the dissolution:

> *I herewith offer Twenty Five Guineas for the Right to trade on the name of D. & W. Auchterlonie. It is a condition, as I made clear in our phone messages, that access to the Sales Ledger of the said firm be accorded me and that I can use the stamps or other marks of the above Firm.*

Another telltale item of interest is seen in a letter from the solicitors handling the bankruptcy matter for the D. & W. Auchterlonie firm. After legal fees, the disbursements of remaining funds was made. Tom Auchterlonie had claims against both David and Willie, personally, to the amounts of 4/5 (four shillings, five pence) and was awarded one penny from David's estate and eight pence from Willie's estate. Against the firm he had claimed another 4/7 and was awarded two pence. In all he received less than a shilling.

Keith Auchterlonie, Tom's grandson, later in life admitted he had on a couple occasions, when a young boy, innocently entered the D. & W. Auchterlonie shop when Laurie was the proprietor. Had his parents known about these visits, there would have been dire consequences for him.

120

At one point in our conversations, not knowing the reason for there being two Auchterlonie business, I naively asked Eric Auchterlonie for an explanation. His answer was polite and matter of fact, but very short and to the point. "They wouldn't make my father a partner." This was obviously the root of the estrangement between the two factions of the family. In his dialogues with me Eric always referred to his cousin Laurie, the club maker working virtually next door, as "he who shall remain nameless." I remember the occasion when I first heard him use that precise terminology—October 1982. The six Auchterlonie brothers were all deceased. Their sons, the succeeding generation of Auchterlonies, were in their 70s and yet the family feud continued.

The issue of partnership, when it involved Willie Auchterlonie joining his brother David and Andrew Crosthwaite, propelled the brothers into a highly successful business of their own. Partnership, when Tom Auchterlonie asked for his just rewards, ultimately contributed to the demise of David and Willie's firm and an irreparable family rift.

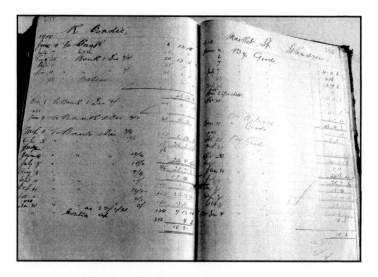

This is the original ledger book where Tom Auchterlonie recorded entries of his sales and purchases. The top pages show his transactions with Robert Condie, the cleek maker on Market Street. The bottom pages recap his business with Tom Stewart of Argyle Street. Both are dated 1919, the first year he was in business. The D. & W. Auchterlonie firm traded extensively with both Condie and Stewart. The fact that both traded with the infant firm of Tom Auchterlonie was a testament to the sound business practices and trustworthiness he established while managing D. & W. Auchterlonie.

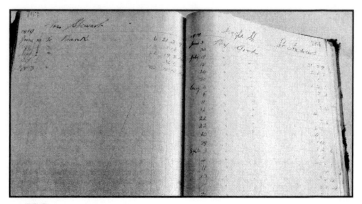

Tom Auchterlonie with waxed moustache ends; an undated photo, possibly circa 1910. Tom always displayed a sartorial flair noticeably absent from his older brothers.

123

The Holing Out Putter

From a product standpoint, there were three milestones for Tom Auchterlonie: the Holing Out Putter, the clubs made for the Japanese Imperial Family and the introduction of the Itz It Itz In clubs.

The first of these, the Holing Out model putter, was patented in 1924. As is seen in the product description, Tom was always very scientific about the nature of his designs. Each facet of the club's construction has a purpose and each facet is explained. This straightforward and logical approach befitted a young man who had run a large business and was meticulous in all his mannerisms including always being handsomely attired.

The club had these characteristics:

- ♦ Vertical Face. Same depth throughout.
- ♦ Broad sole at right angles to face, with weight at bottom and directly at hitting point.
- ♦ Back beveled at toe and heel.
- ♦ Line on back indicating direction of putt.
- ♦ Shaft, Neck and Face all in the same line.
- ♦ Face same depth throughout

This last point meant that the face of the blade was not in line with the center of the hosel diameter, but lined with the front edge of the hosel circumference. The forward placement of the blade virtually eliminated the risk of shanking a putt.

Tom felt the advantages of all this were:

- ▪ This arrangement imparts underspin to the ball, so

124

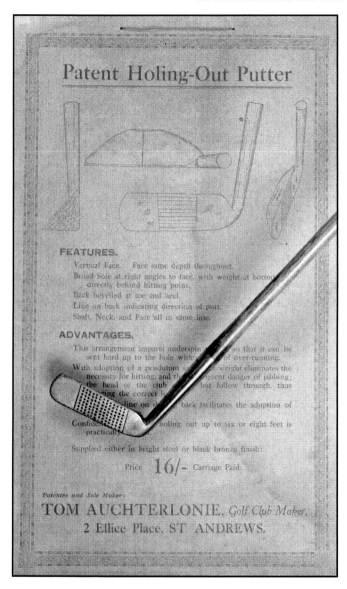

A cardboard advertising broadside for the Holing Out Putter intended to be hung in the shop of any and all club professionals. The club came with a dot or line face pattern.

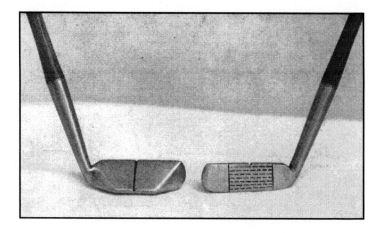

The Holing Out Putter from an old Auchterlonie display photo.

that it can be sent hard upward to the hole without fear of over-running.

- With adoption of a pendulum swing the weight eliminates the necessity of hitting, and the consequent danger of jabbing; the head of the club cannot but follow through, thus insuring the correct line.

- The directing line on sloping back facilitated the adoption of the right stance.

- Confident results and holing out up to six or eight feet is practically assured.

The Holing Out Putter is normally found in Waverly (regular) steel, and when first introduced it could also be obtained in black bronze finish. Eventually, it came out in rustless steel, too. The face markings could be dots, hyphens or lines.

The club was successful in terms of sales. One of Tom's ads stated that over 5,000 were sold the first year*. That's a lot of clubs at 16/- each (sixteen shillings). It was his first success in the area of club design or invention and it brought immediate recognition to his young firm.

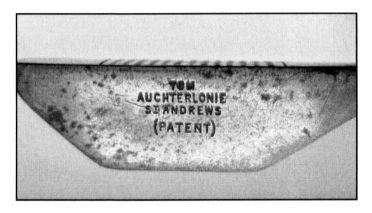

Above: The markings on the sole of the Holing Out Putter.

Below: The club front showing the face flush with the edge of the hosel and the notch where hosel meets blade.

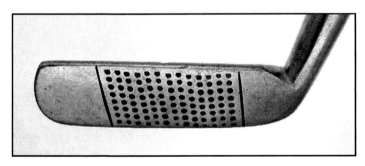

*Note: An article in *The Sports Trades Journal*, August, 1924 says that Tom sold 6,000 Holing Out putters in the first year.

127

"ARDEN,"
ESHE ROAD,
BLUNDELLSANDS,
LIVERPOOL, 23.

19th May 1941.

Tom Auchterlonie Esq.,
St. Andrews,
SCOTLAND.

Dear Sir,

I had the pleasure of playing golf yesterday with one of the 'deadliest' putters I have ever played against.

He was using one of your putters, which I have tried to describe on the enclosed form.

Have you one of these putters available.

If you have, you may either send it to me C.O.D. or write to me informing me of the price, when I will send you a remittance.

Yours faithfully,
SYDNEY HILL.

This is one of the many testimonial letters Tom received during his business career. The writer went to great lengths to accurately sketch the Holing Out Putter.

Reverse side =>

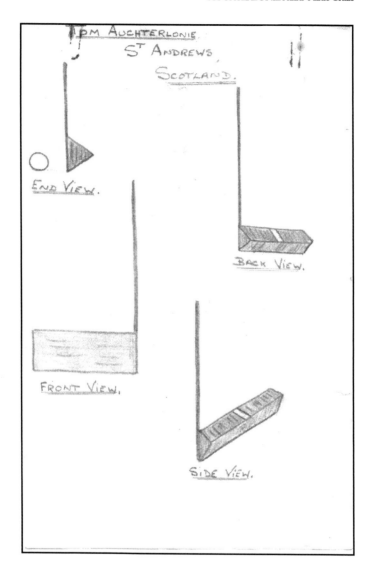

Peter Georgiady

Two *advertisements for the Holing Out Putter:*

Top: Golfers Handbook, *1922; with unusual sideways text;*

Bottom: Golfing, *May, 1924*

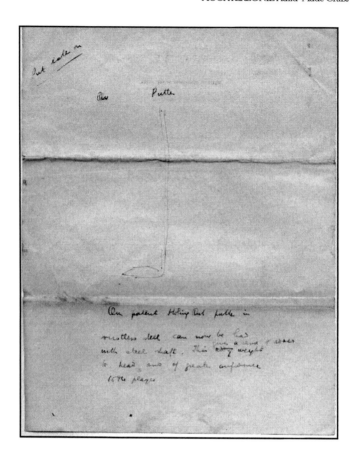

Tom Auchterlonie hand wrote this draft of an advertisement for the Holing Out Putter's conversion to steel shaft and sketched a primitive golf club.

"Our Holing Out Putter in rustless steel can now be had with steel shaft. This gives a sense of added weight to the head and of greater confidence to the player.

The front side of this draft read: **"The Steel Age in Golf"**

The Imperial Japanese Golf Clubs

In 1926, Tom was contacted by a business agent working in Japan, Mr. Uchida. The agent had connections to the Imperial Family of Japan who wished to order golf clubs. The order comprised some six sets of clubs to be used by the Imperial Family and their friends, guests and fellow members of the Nagasaki Golf Club.

Being an expert club maker, Tom and his staff were able to make clubs to an appropriate fit without the luxury of personally seeing the users. Height and weight measurements were sent by letter and the clubs constructed according to the mail order specifications. Prince Kuni (age 50), for instance, was only 5 foot tall and 100 pounds. His wife, Princess Kuni was only 80 pounds in weight. With patrons of that small stature the clubs Tom made must have been almost juvenile in size. But the large size of the order meant all sizes of clubs were to be built to fit the wide range of people who would receive them.

The only known club extant from these sets is an ivory faced driver in the "De-Luxe" series. Additionally, it is stamped with a simple chrysanthemum blossom mark above the Tom Auchterlonie name. The length of the club is 41", possibly a bit too long for the shorter members of the Imperial Family, so it was probably one intended for the retinue.

Tom also was very astute to ask for permission to use terminology in his advertising that stated he was patronized by the Imperial Family of Japan. This was eventually granted and that wording appears on his price

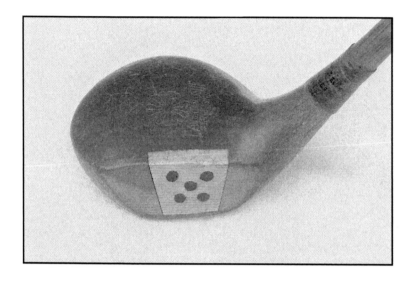

The ivory faced driver referred to in the letter ordering clubs for the Japanese Imperial Family started as one of Tom's top of the line "De-Luxe" model wooden clubs. An extra thick ivory insert was added and the club was completed with the application of the hand rubbed heirloom finish. What distinguished these clubs from any of the other special order clubs was the use of the chrysanthemum blossom mark signifying the Imperial Japanese designation.

133

list and several advertisements. The 1926 order was followed with a second order for additional clubs in 1929. The very carefully guarded nature of the lives of the Imperial Family made this order most unusual and a great honor for Tom and his workmen. To have received a second order unquestionably meant that his workmanship, and the discrete manner in which he handled the business, won approval of the Imperial Family.

A curious incident occurred in 1935 when a Japanese Naval Officer played golf in New Zealand with an expatriated Scotsman named Alexander Robertson. The Japanese Officer was playing with Tom Auchterlonie golf clubs presented to him by the Imperial family. Alex Robertson had been employed by Tom Auchterlonie and had been one of the craftsmen assigned to producing the Japanese order. He had since emigrated to New Zealand and taken a position as a golf club professional.

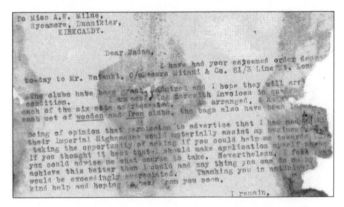

In this typed letter to Miss A.W. Milne, one of the persons that facilitated the club order, Tom asks, "**Being of opinion that permission to advertise that I made clubs for their Imperial Highnesses would materially assist my business, I'm taking the opportunity of asking if you could help me towards that...**

His answer came in the letter shown on the next page.

134

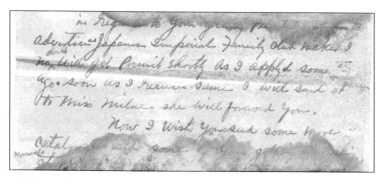

*A portion of a return letter received by Tom following the
arrival of the clubs in Japan reads:*

"I thank you for ....your clubs made for Japanese Imperial Family. I had
the honor to ask you to do the work. The clubs all made good quality
balance good ...fact satisfactory to the Imperial Family and other members
of the Nagasaki Golf Club. Now again H.I.H. directs me to order one more
set.....wishes me to order..."

"in regard to your getting privilege to advertise as Japanese Imperial family
club maker I no doubt will get permit shortly as I applied some time ago.
Soon as I receive same I will send it to Miss Milne, she will forward you.

Now I wish you send some of your golfing and teaching manuals....."

*The answer here may have been conditional but based on the
wording on future brochures and ads he was given permission.*

Royal patronage of Scotland's golf club makers was an institution for centuries dating back four hundred years. Robert Forgan's relationship with H.R.H. The Prince of Wales is the most notable example. The order received from Japan's Imperial Family at Tom's created both public interest and increased market visibility. The clubs made for the Emperor and his retinue were on display in Tom's shop window where they drew many interested onlookers. It would be safe to assume that most of these special Imperial clubs have been lost, either as a result of the ravages of war or the discarding of old equipment over time. This driver could possibly be the last remaining Imperial Japanese club.

136

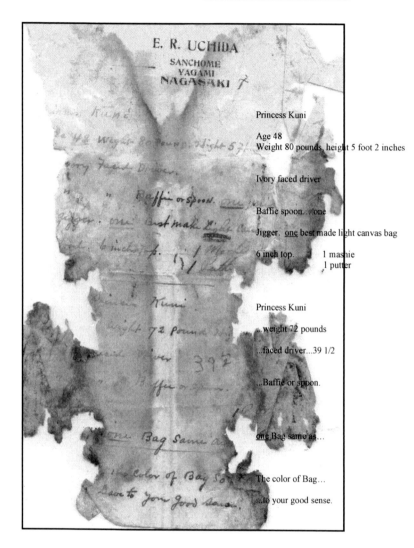

E. R. UCHIDA
SANCHOME
YAGAMI
NAGASAKI

Princess Kuni

Age 48
Weight 80 pounds, height 5 foot 2 inches

Ivory faced driver

Baffie spoon...one

Jigger, one best made light canvas bag

6 inch top.   1 mashie
                     1 putter

Princess Kuni

...weight 72 pounds

...faced driver...39 1/2

...Baffie or spoon.

one Bag same as...

The color of Bag...

...to your good sense.

These pages are part of the hand written order for the Imperial Japanese golf clubs detailing the physical characteristics of the persons to receive the clubs and the type of clubs requested for each set.

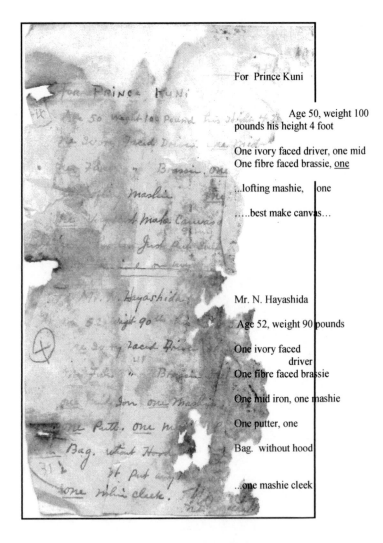

For Prince Kuni

Age 50, weight 100 pounds his height 4 foot

One ivory faced driver, one mid
One fibre faced brassie, <u>one</u>

...lofting mashie, one

.....best make canvas...

Mr. N. Hayashida

Age 52, weight 90 pounds

One ivory faced driver

One fibre faced brassie

One mid iron, one mashie

One putter, one

Bag. without hood

...one mashie cleek

Unfortunately these notes and other letters concerning the Imperial club order suffered water damage over the years and are only partially readable.

"ITZIT" Club Series

Tom Auchterlonie's greatest accomplishment was the design and introduction of the ITZ IT ITZ IN irons. They represent one of the most advanced club designs of their day and can certainly be considered as the first truly modern golf irons. With a design patent granted in 1925, number 715118, they hit the market as Tom's highest grade of club.

The design is detailed in Tom's own words in the accompanying display box which, succinctly explained, the ITZIT irons were the first round-soled iron with cambered flange. They have an exceptionally fine balance to them and feel as good today as any modern club, a testament to the harmony of head, shaft and grip.

As a set, they did not include successively numerical irons. Rather, a player could build a set from a selection of four "Irons," three "Mashies," a Lofter, a Niblick and Putters. Initially only irons were available but woods were eventually introduced as well. The success of the pattern prompted Tom to also make extra clubs like jiggers and sammies.

In terms of competition, the new 'sets' of matched irons that hit the market at roughly the same time were primitive in design when compared to the ITZ IT-ITZ IN. Spalding's Kro-Flite irons were sets in evolution until the famous black face series was introduced in 1927. George Nicoll made headlines with his Indicator series in 1926 but much of the work was done to standardize the shaft specifications rather than to tinker with the shape of the head, which was pretty standard 1920s fare.

139

Golfing, August 1927

A Word About Clubs

We hear that Tom Auchterlonie, the well known St Andrews golf club-maker, is doing extraordinarily well with his new range of irons, to which he has given the name of the "Itzit" clubs. The chief features which are peculiar to the "Itzit" clubs are :--

Firstly, One-sixth of the sole at the heel and toe is rounded off so that the remaining two-thirds of the sole lie flat on the ground. This allows the club to clear or get through without tripping on the toe or the heel.

Secondly, The edges of the back and the front of the sole are also rounded off. This improvement makes it almost impossible to dig heavily, or the club to trip on the back edge, thus giving the club an uninterrupted follow through. On account of this rounded edge, the ball, though topped, is not hacked.

Thirdly, The blade is also fashioned so that the top edge is longer than the sole. This makes it easy to get direction from the long top edge.

Fourthly, The blade is cleaned out at the heel so that the ball can be heeled without being shanked, and in order to eliminate the feeling of a heeled ball, extra weight is worked into the back of the club at the heel.

Fifthly, The top back edge of the blade is beveled away so that a good sighting line is provided.

Sixthly, There is a longitudinal bulb along the bottom of the sole which has the affect of putting a quick stop or underspin on the ball.

Seventhly, The clubs are shafted with very select sticks, with superior cone shaped calf skin grips.

Make and workmanship, it is hardly necessary to add, are in every way worthy of the reputation of the inventor.

Around ten years after the introduction of the ITZIT irons, Tom was on the brink of a patent infringement action. Several manufacturers had copied the style of the ITZIT irons with its rounded flange sole. The matter was brought to Tom's attention in a letter written early in 1937 where it was intimated that Thornton's, the large India rubber manufacturers with retail stores in Glasgow and Edinburgh, were selling obvious copies of the ITZIT irons, made by Ben Sayers, Jr. That letter also mentioned that clubs designed by Enid Wilson for Gradidge (sold through Lillywhite's of Piccadilly Circus), and Bobby Jones's irons also had round soles after the Auchterlonie pattern.

Years ago it was not uncommon for shops in St Andrews to give out scorecards embellished with ads, for the town's golf courses.

Tom Auchterlonie used that opportunity to promote his ITZIT clubs noting they were the product of 'golfer-craftsmen,' that is, club makers who were also good golfers.

This card dates from after 1934, when they moved to Golf Place but before 1957 when the Road Hole at the Old Course changed from a short par 5 to a long par 4. Notice the 6" stymie measure.

Improve Your Game
With
TOM AUCHTERLONIE'S
IT IT
IT IN
GOLF CLUBS.

There's nothing like an ITZIT—their special designs are the result of long experience and experiment by player-craftsmen. Each Club is HAND made throughout by one expert. Get one into your hands and realise "It's IT"!

Beware of Imitations
• Clubs That Make Golfers. •

Tom Auchterlonie
2 GOLF PLACE
THE CORNER SHOP
TELEPHONE 253. **ST. ANDREWS**

If Tom took any legal action it is not public knowledge. Many manufacturers' clubs were beginning to successfully adopt a more sculptured look with complex patterns of weight displacement and it may have been very difficult to protect the design.

With the wholesale switch from wood shafts to steel shafts following the R & A acceptance in 1929 Tom continued to make ITZIT clubs with steel shafts into the 1930s and 1940s. The original 1925 patent was valid for five years with the option for two additional five year extensions. The second extension was granted in 1935 the same year Tom applied for a patent on a 2-sided chipping iron with steel shaft as part of the ITZIT family.

The allowance of non-wood shafts was made by the U.S.G.A. in 1924 and American golfers had been playing with steel shafts since then, though wood shafts were still the dominant material until the early 1930s. Many sets were sold with steel shafted woods but the irons were still being fitted with hickory shafts. However, by 1930, most of the top level American professional golfers had converted to metal shafts. In Britain, golfers had to wait until the R & A's 1929 ruling to use metal shafts. Change also came more slowly there and well into the 1930s, wood shaft clubs were still available on a wide spread basis. In 1935 this verbiage appeared in a story about the Tom Auchterlonie business.

> *"Notwithstanding the altered conditions created by the introduction of steel shafts, our friend still continues to receive many orders for hickory-shafted clubs, and favors the belief of many that it is not improbable that hickory will again come into its own."*
>
> *Golf Monthly, August 1935*

142

Tom Moves West

With business prospering, the Ellice Place facility that had been Tom's bastion for over 15 years was finally deemed to be too small. A site at the corner of Golf Place and Pilmour Links, strategically situated just yards away from the Old Course starter's box and within sight of the course, became available when the St Andrews Golf Club* vacated it in order to move to larger quarters. The building was offered at a price of £1,800 and drew no takers. When it was again offered for sale at £1,000 Tom put in an offer, which was accepted. By August of 1934, Tom had moved his business to 2 Pilmour Links and the family had moved into the living quarters above the shop. Coincidentally, it also placed him two doors away from D. & W. Auchterlonie, the site of the shop here he had worked for his brothers for over twenty years. Undoubtedly to further assist in differentiating his shop from that of his brothers, Tom started referring to it in his advertising as "The Corner Shop."

Some years later, the business next door on Golf Place, MacArthur's Bakery removed to South Street and Tom bought that property as well, expanding his shop again. This expanded facility now afforded him two storefronts facing Golf Place, the route to the golf courses from the North Street corridor and the railway station.

It was also at this time that the old D. & W. Auchterlonie firm was being dissolved. At the end of 1934, Tom contacted the solicitors handling the disposition of the old firm and offered the sum of 25 guineas for the rights to

* *The Golf Trader*, April 1934 states the building was the quarters of the St. Andrews Artisan Golf Club.

trade under the D. & W. Auchterlonie name, the sales ledger and possession of their marks and stamps. This arrangement never came to fruition and there continued to be two Auchterlonie firms and two shops in St Andrews for the next fifty years.

Although the retail shop at the corner of Pilmour Links and Golf Place was a vast improvement for Tom's operations, much of the actual club making work was performed off site, in a workshop on Fleming Place.

Tom Auchterlonie moved from Ellice Place to the "Corner Shop" at Pilmour Links and Golf Place in 1934. The shop was considerably larger than his first premises and more modern in appearance. The biggest advantage was the fact that virtually everyone coming from the train station would walk past the shop, down Golf Place, to get to the golf courses. The firm remained in these quarters for over 50 years. A shop bearing the Auchterlonie name is located there today.

144

The Workshop

When I was a boy in the late 50s and early 60s, wooden clubs were made, and iron clubs assembled, in what was always referred to simply as 'the workshop.'

This was a self contained factory building located in Fleming Place, to the south side of St Andrews, about ¾ of a mile from the main shop premises. It was just around the corner from Park Street, the small street where my grandfather Tom had a house built in the early 1900s and where my father, Eric, was born and brought up.

This must have been a bustling place in the heyday of the firm's manufacturing era. By the time that I am recounting, the volume of manufacturing had diminished significantly and I only ever remember 3 or 4 club makers working there, supplemented from time to time by my father who, I suspect, enjoyed this aspect of the business more than any other.

Above and following page: The Tom Auchterlonie workshop at Fleming Place, 1924.

Of course, by now, the steel shaft had to all intents and purposes completely replaced hickory, although there was a small residual demand for wooden shafted putters. Some wooden heads were still made from persimmon, imported from the USA, but the majority of club heads were now being made from laminated blocks. I remember my father lamenting that persimmon of decent quality was virtually impossible to get hold of, although he did have a very small horde of old sawn persimmon in the wood shed to the rear of the workshop. In the past, this would have been full of wood for shafts and heads.

The wood for most heads was bought in as very roughly shaped long blocks and would be roughly shaped on a large band-saw. From pictures I have seen that date back to the 1930s, I would say that this band-saw had been in continual use since that time.

Next, the roughly shaped blocks would be placed two at a time into a copying lathe, where they would be shaped using a metal master.

146

The band saws at the Fleming Place workshop.

After this, the process became less industrial and more craft based. The neck of the club would be drilled out for the shaft and fine adjustments to shape, lie, and loft would be made using hand files and scrapers. Rebates for the face and sole plates would be cut with a router. The club head would then be shafted (the word had no other connotations in these days, at least not in St Andrews), cut to length and more adjustments made to the lie.

Lead was then often added, either under the sole plate or behind the face plate – an activity that involved melting scrap lead in a cast iron ladle over an open gas flame, and then pouring the molten metal into a hole that had been drilled in the head. Of course, there were no concerns about lead poisoning in these days and if you got a small burn from a splash of molten lead, that was just part of the risks that one took in coming to work.

The club head would then be finished, by staining and multiple coats of a shellac based varnish, rubbed down

147

between coats with steel wool.

Finally, whipping, a tar covered twine would be wound round the neck to strengthen it and finish things off neatly. For a young boy, this was one of the most fascinating parts of the whole process and used what I presume was a tool that had been developed by the club makers especially for the task. Supremely simple, it consisted just of about a six inch length of wooden dowel, probably an offcut from a hickory shaft, with a rounded notch cut in the top. This would be held vertically in the vice and the bobbin of whipping twine put over it. The club maker would then pull out just the right length of twine for the club – no rulers or guides were used, this was something that he knew from experience – and the twine looped around the dowel, above the bobbin, to keep any more from unravelling. With the end of the twine held against the neck of the club, the twine would be pulled taught. The club maker would then stick the club under his arm and, rolling it horizontally, work back towards the vice, feeding the twine onto the neck, whilst keeping the twine taught. When the twine was all on the neck, it would be finished off and then, rolled flat using the notch in the top of the stick. Try as I might, I could never master this seemingly simple job.

I suspect that much of the process was unchanged from how

A view of the timber drying sheds in Fleming Place.

it had been when my grandfather first set up in business. With the exception of the turning machine, which was obviously a more recent addition, the machines were all driven by belts that were themselves driven from cams which in, turn were driven by main belts, driven from a central electric motor. These belts were completely unprotected and would certainly not have escaped the attention of today's factory inspectors.

Some of the clubs were made for shop stock or for a small remaining wholesale trade. However, much of the production was to customer order and these clubs were tailor made to individual customer requirements. As well as details of finish and grip, the clubs were fitted in much the same way as a Saville Row tailor would fit a suit, ensuring that they met the needs of the customer or, sometimes, what the customer, against all advice, perceived as his needs.

The level of production by now was a fraction of what it had been some 20 or 30 years before. Mass advertising had come into the world of golf and, increasingly, production was being dominated by the large, industrial manufacturers. Whilst their product was certainly no better and they could not offer the level of customised production, they were winning the hearts and minds of customers through the endorsements of the champions of the day, a strategy that exactly

The copying lathe, for turning wooden club heads from a pattern.

149

mirrored some of the early D. & W. Auchterlonie advertising. That the clubs used by many of the stars of the day bore little resemblance to the ones in the shops that bore their name made little difference in the eyes of the golfing public.

As a boy I had no real knowledge of the market but, looking back with the benefits of my own business experience, it seems that a more aggressive, self-confident approach to this competition might have been successful in ensuring the long term future of the craftsman led St Andrews club making tradition. Instead of hitting back by emphasising the exclusivity, the tradition, and the bespoke nature of the product and re-establishing a truly up-market brand, the clubs were sold at a significantly lower price than the mass produced clubs that were their competition, probably devaluing them in the eyes of the consumer.

With manufacturing volumes declining further, the Fleming Place factory was closed in the mid sixties and sold to a local glazing firm. A small workshop was established in the Pilmour Links premises and the two remaining clubmakers, Alick and Dougie Roland moved up to work there until their retirement. Two more club makers, Frank Thom and, after he left to take up employment outside the golf trade, Sandy Smith were recruited from other local firms to carry on the making and repair of a small number of clubs. Finally, before the sale of the business, Patrick Kinsley, a distant cousin of Eric, joined the firm as an apprentice and learned the trade, becoming the last club maker in the family.

The Fleming Place workshop continued in a number of roles until it was finally demolished in 2005 and a number of flats built on the site.

Keith Auchterlonie

For a number of years, the Firm of D. & W. Brodie, in neighboring Anstruther, was the forge for many of Tom Auchterlonie's iron club heads. Quite probably the

Brodies made the ITZIT series for many years as the intimation of a special business relationship can be sensed in the patent infringement letter sent to Tom by David Brodie. Sometime in the 1950s Tom bought the Brodie forge and continued to make his iron club heads in Anstruther.

The Anstruther Cleek Factory

In an early example of vertical integration, the family had bought the established Anstruther cleek making firm of D. & W. Brodie in the 1950s.

This was sited on the northern edge of the town, some 8 miles from St Andrews. My father would visit the factory regularly to handle paperwork, collect finished heads for the St Andrews workshop and, generally, keep a proprietorial eye on things. I often managed to persuade him to make these visits after school had finished for the day so that I could accompany him. This was less out of an interest in the workings of the factory on my part and more to do with the fact that one of the best Italian ice cream makers in Scotland was based on the harbour front at Anstruther.

To a boy, entering the cleek works was a little bit like entering another world. Unlike the dusty, but clean, light and relatively quiet workshop in St Andrews where the wooden clubs were made, this was a true engineering factory environment of noise, darkness, smells and dirt. The cleek makers also seemed to come from a different world – harder and tougher, although I never experienced anything other than friendship and tolerance of a little boy getting under their feet.

Apart from the office, which was dominated by a large wooden desk, the factory floor was split into two distinct areas. You came in off the street into the finishing shop. Here, the newly forged iron heads would have their hosels drilled out, be stamped and polished and have their faces scored and sandblasted. The smell of cutting oil and polishing wax filled the air, the benches where the drilling was carried out were covered in metal scarf – great fun to play with – and everything, from the earth floor up, was filthy.

However, it was the further half of the factory that stands out in my memory. This was where the two large upright presses which shaped the new iron heads were. They stood upright, looking black and dangerous – as indeed, they were. Anybody getting their arm in the way of the press as it came down with its tremendous force on the blank would, at best, be a hospital case. These presses did not run continuously, although they may have done so in earlier years. When they did, however, they were extremely noisy but it was the menacing appearance of them that stays in my mind to this day.

Keith Auchterlonie

When the Golf Place facility was remodeled in 1967, the *Evening Telegraph* reported that a club-making work room was added to the lower level and that it was heated and cooled to make working on clubs feasible at any time of the year. This might seem like an unusual statement but historically, workers in club making facilities were subjected to very primitive conditions. The floors were usually packed dirt, lighting wasn't good and there was little in the way of climate control, save opening a window or two. The space was normally very hot in the summer, especially where there was a forge, and bitterly cold in the late fall and winter months. For a club maker, Eric's new facility was luxurious.

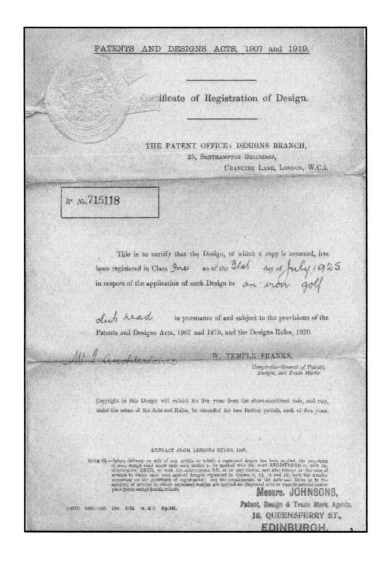

Design Registration number 715118 was granted to Tom Auchterlonie's iron golf club head design, which was sold under the ITZIT brand name, July 31, 1925.

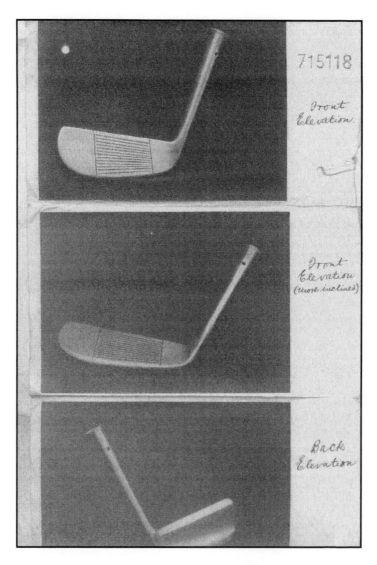

Tom submitted three photo views of his ITZ IT design which emphasized the club's rounded and cambered flange sole. These photos were undoubtedly taken by a professional photographer.

154

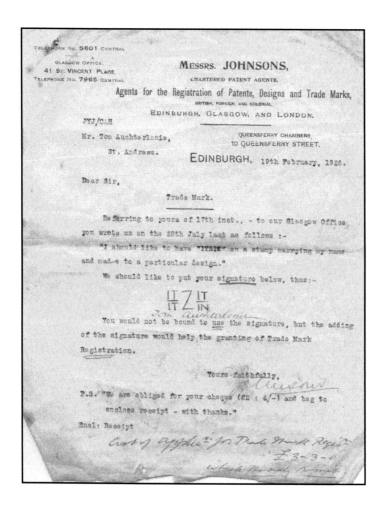

This was step two of the protection process Tom went through for the ITZIT irons. After registering the design, he filed application for a trademark on the logo for the ITZIT clubs at a cost of £3-3-0 (three guineas) in February, 1926.

155

Class 49—continued.

Registration of this Trade Mark shall give no right to the exclusive use of the word " Itzit " or of the word " Itzin."

468,550. Golf Clubs. TOM AUCHTERLONIE, 2, Ellice Place, St. Andrews, Scotland; Golf Club Maker.—27th March, 1926.

The above listing was published in the May 19, 1926 Trade Marks Journal, *which displayed all the trade marks recently receiving registration approval. From the letter on the opposite page, Tom contacted his patent agents in July the prior year on the topic of trade marking his ITZ IT ITZ IN mark. He apparently reminded them in mid-February. They recommended adding his signature to the mark to make it easier to gain approval (since, as the listing shows, the words Itzit and Itzin had no exclusivity for Auchterlonie or the product). The trade mark was granted fairly quickly afterward, March 27, appearing in the* Trade Marks Journal *eight weeks later.*

Advertisement for the ITZIT line of clubs, however the trademark was incorrectly pictured (it should have been ITZIT, ITZIN). From Golfing, *1927, it makes sure there is a mention of Tom's patronage by the Imperial Family of Japan.*

Tom Auchterlonie—Above: in about 1950.
Below: taking a stroll on the pavement in front of the shop
on the occasion of his 80th birthday in 1959.

The Clubs of Tom Auchterlonie

The byword for the golf club output from the Tom Auchterlonie firm was 'quality.' Tom learned that when he worked for his brothers. After he opened his own business, he carried that principle even further. He wanted his name to be associated with the highest quality implements available to golfers and he achieved this end.

> *The hand-made wooden clubs turned out by this firm are renowned the world over for their beautiful design, finish and balance, and no matter what pattern finds favor, Tom Auchterlonie and his workmen are capable of fashioning and embodying the minutest detail. Strangely enough in these days when the demand has increased for cheap clubs, Tom Auchterlonie has rarely been approached to supply such clubs, and, naturally, he has never identified himself with the production of cheap articles. His high-class hand made clubs have been exported to all parts of the world where, according to numerous unsolicited testimonials, they appear to give universal satisfaction.*

> *Golf Monthly, August 1935*

Interestingly enough, at a time when the wood shaft era was truly at an end, that same *Golf Monthly* review stated that hickory shafted clubs were still available from Tom's shop. With the R and A finally sanctioning non-wood shafts in 1929, a full five years after the USGA allowed the same, and with the British being less inclined to quickly depart from old ways, wood shafts were still highly visible up until golf activity subsided at wartime. In the U.S. virtually all wood shafts were gone from sale room shelves by 1931.

This ad from Golfing, 1926 leaves little doubt about the quality of Tom Auchterlonie's products.

159

Tom Auchterlonie Early Clubs

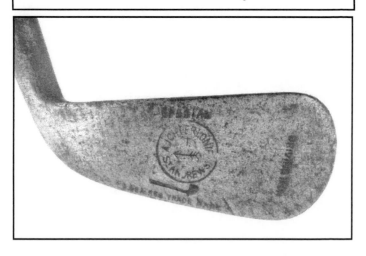

The first irons sold by Tom Auchterlonie's new shop were marked with his name and a small arrow in a circle. These two clubs are very similar—a driving iron (top) and a cleek (bottom). The top was made by Tom Stewart's forge, marked with the famous pipe; the lower example by Robert Condie and marked with his rose. Circa 1920.

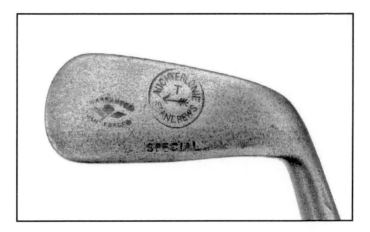

Tom Auchterlonie Early Clubs

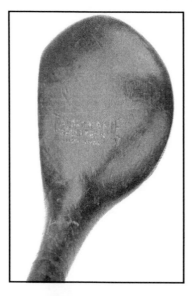

The general date range for the transition from splice head woods to socket head woods is roughly 1900-1910. This Tom Auchterlonie splice head driver could only be made after 1919 since that is the year Tom went into business. It illustrates that some golfers were slow to change and a good club maker could accommodate the preferences of any customer.

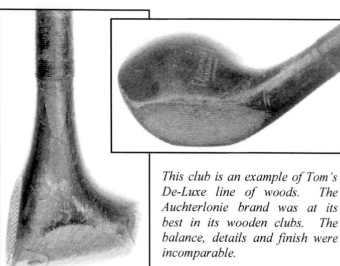

This club is an example of Tom's De-Luxe line of woods. The Auchterlonie brand was at its best in its wooden clubs. The balance, details and finish were incomparable.

161

The "Ellice" Model Clubs

Tom Auchterlonie had a three—tiered product line and The "Ellice" brandclubs were the economy models. However he referred to them as "high grade clubs at a low grade price." The name came from the shop's address at Ellice Place, leaving no confusion with his brothers' rival firm. Above—two views of a stripe top driver; bottom—a bent neck blade putter.

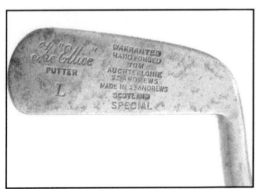

The Special Model Clubs

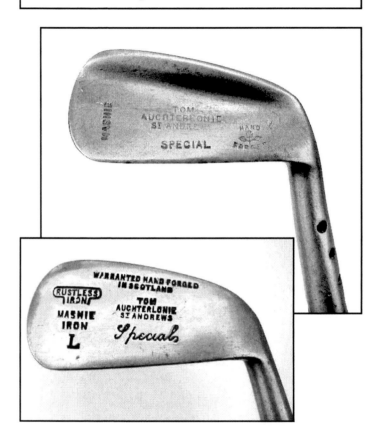

*Top: The Condie forge produced this Maxwell Pattern mashie.
The pattern consisted of the flange sole and the holed drilled in
the hosel. The Tom Auchterlonie catalog specified that Maxwell
pattern clubs cost   an extra 6 d. (six   pence) over regular
models.*

*Bottom: Tom Auchterlonie mashie iron in rustless steel.   The
markings suggest the head was made by Brodie or Nicoll.*

The Special Model Clubs

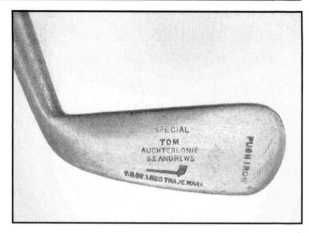

A push iron made by Tom Stewart was basically used for punch or 'knock down' shots.

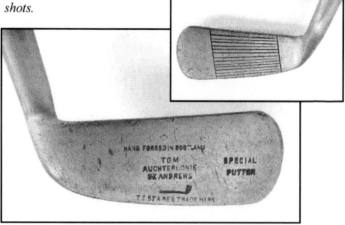

Tom Auchterlonie bent neck, line face blade putter with Tom Stewart marks. The Special series was the mid-priced range of clubs. Tom charged an extra 1/- (one shilling) for Stewart-made heads.

164

The Special Model Clubs

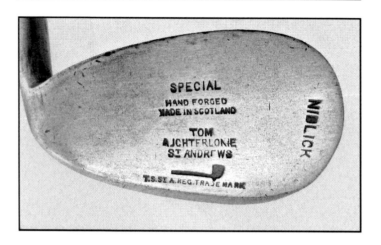

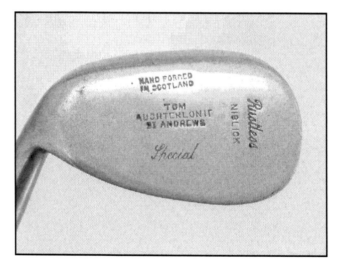

Two niblicks made about ten years apart: The top example is typical Tom Stewart fare. The bottom example probably comes from the Nicoll forge in Leven.

Wooden Putter

St. Andrews has always been known for club makers who continued to produce wooden putters long after they had fallen out of fashion elsewhere. The club at right and below, showing beech grain banding, has lost its original finish but the tapered T and E are still visible. This mark was used until 1926 when the signature, seen on the bottom photos, took it's place.

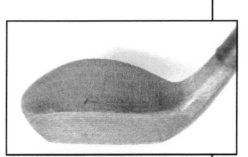

The ITZIT Series Clubs

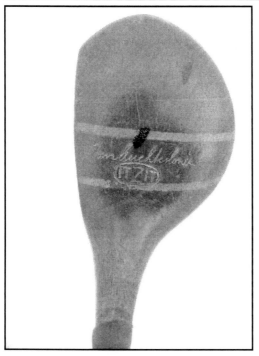

Crown and sole views of the Tom Auchterlonie ITZIT model driver. The club came in a unique stripe top finish with two narrow horizontal stripes (which the Auchterlonie catalog described as 'bars'). The oval ITZIT mark was unique to the woods and never appeared on the irons. Normally, in wooden clubs, the driver had no sole plate. In this series, all wood clubs were fitted with the same shape plate for continuity.

167

The ITZIT Series Clubs

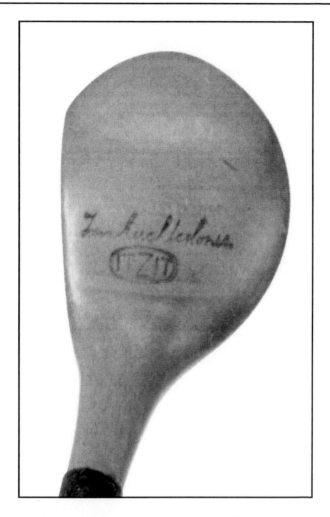

A brassie from the ITZIT series that has been refinished. Traces of the original stripe top finish remain but the Tom Auchterlonie signature is more visible on this refinished piece.

168

The ITZIT Series Clubs

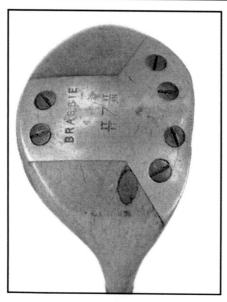

Above: The sole of the ITZIT model brassie showing the T-shaped sole plate and the ITZIT trademark.

Below: Views of the crown and sole plate of the spoon..

169

The ITZIT Series Clubs

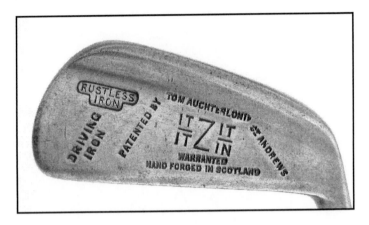

The driving iron for the ITZIT series was not one of the original clubs and was introduced a few years after the first clubs in the series were brought out.

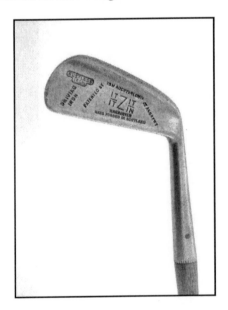

The ITZIT Series Clubs

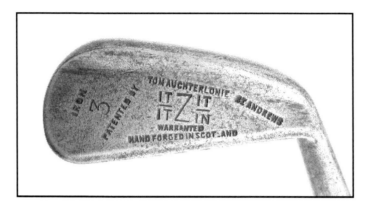

The ITZIT series didn't offer sequentially lofted irons. Numbered irons as we know them today were still being formulated when these clubs were designed. Golfers had the choice in the ITZIT series of an "Iron" in a 1, 2, 3 or 4 pattern, each with a slightly different weight. This is the Iron 3 in standard Waverly steel.

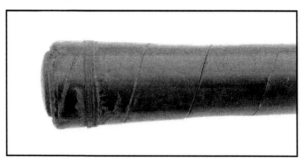

One other feature standard on all ITZIT series clubs was the 'bell end grip.' The wrap was made from specially selected black calf leather—the "T.A. Grip"— and tapered out at the butt end for gripping comfort, something available on most clubs today.

171

The ITZIT Series Clubs

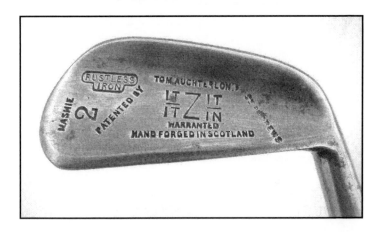

The ITZIT mashie came in three styles—Mashie 1, 2, and 3.. The number 3 mashie (below) had a deeper face and a thinner blade than the number 2 mashie (shown above). The loft is close to being the same, but both are more lofted than the average mashie of the day. With its deep face, the number 3 mashie is close to a spade mashie in form.

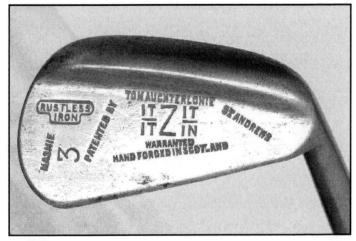

The ITZIT Series Clubs

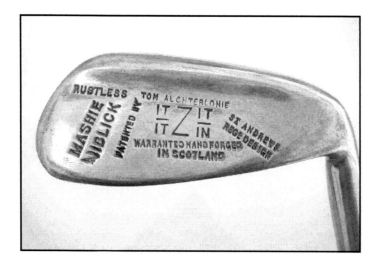

Above: The ITZIT mashie niblick was very rounded in the toe. It was a thicker, heavier club head than the mashies.

Below: The ITZIT putter had the same barrel sole as the irons.

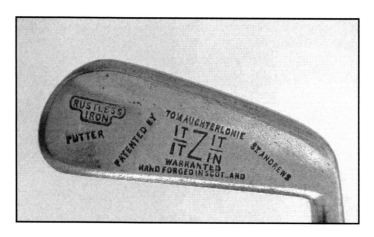

The ITZIT Series Clubs

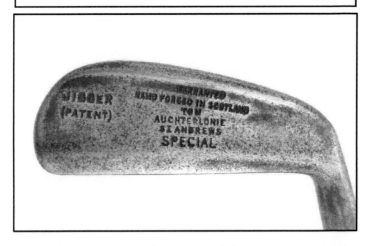

The difference between the jigger and the sammy irons in the ITZIT series can be seen here. The jigger has more of a toe-to-heel rounded sole, the sammy a flatter sole. The jigger also has more loft, a broader sole, a flatter lie and a shorter shaft. The jigger shown above does not carry the ITZIT markings but has all the features of that series, and is marked "Patent." It may be a prototype or a design model that preceded the actual granting of the patent.

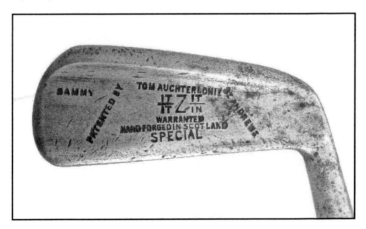

The ITZIT Series Clubs

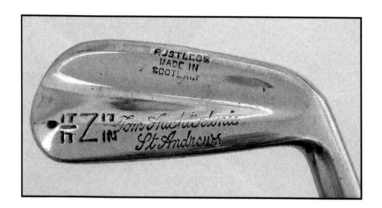

Above: In the 1950s the design of the ITZIT irons changed to reflect a more modern appearance. The new pattern was more like the duo-flange clubs coming from Wilson and Spalding.

Below: All ITZIT irons were faced with a simple line pattern.

Tom Auchterlonie Clubs

Three irons from the Tom Auchterlonie series, the economy line of clubs that debuted in the late 1920s. By the mid-1920s, much of Tom's line was being offered in rustless steel.

Tom Auchterlonie Clubs

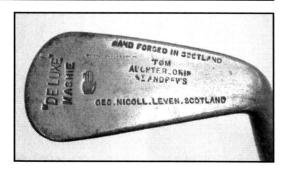

Top: George Nicoll began making club heads for Tom in the 1920s. By the 1950s, they were supplying most of his irons.
Middle: William Gibson (the Star mark) also became a supplier to Tom in the 1920s.
Bottom: The majority of Stewart heads sold to Tom didn't carry the Stewart oval mark, only the pipe.

177

Tom Auchterlonie Clubs

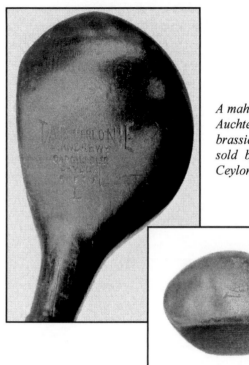

A mahogany stained Tom Auchterlonie socket head brassie in ladies size sold by Cargill & Co., Ceylon.

This shaft mark appears on virtually all Tom Auchterlonie clubs. His mark always included the initial "T," in contrast to the mark used by his brothers' firm, which employed no first initial.

Tom Auchterlonie Clubs (Modern)

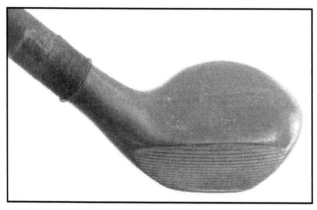

A left handed splice head driver made by Eric Auchterlonie, in his retirement around 1987-88. In form, the only aspect of this club that might give a clue that it was not at least 90 years old would be the "Tom Auchterlonie" decal on the crown.

The Tom Auchterlonie juvenile sized sand iron that Eric made for Bryan Georgiady in 1982.

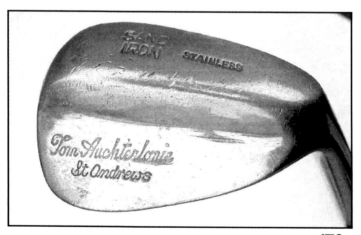

Tom Auchterlonie Two-Faced Chipper

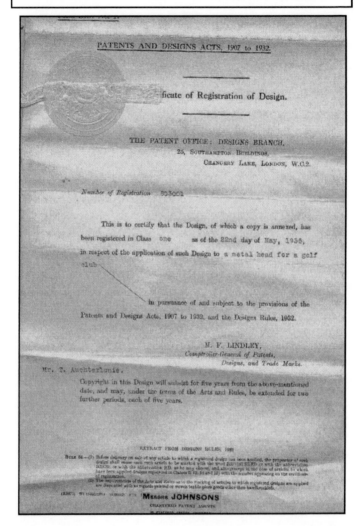

The cover sheet of the Design Registration granted to Tom Auchterlonie for his two-faced chipper. It protected his invention for a period of five years with the option for two five year renewals as well.

180

Tom Auchterlonie Two-Faced Chipper

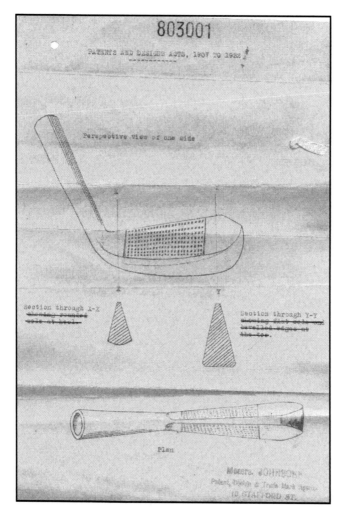

This design drawing was part of the design registration application paperwork for Tom Auchterlonie's two-faced chipper in 1935.

Tom Auchterlonie Clubs

With regard to your Registering your new Design for the Sole
of a Golf Club with Lines or Furrows (Grooves) running at any angle
other than at Right Angles to the Face - we should say that such
Registration could be got if you supply us with clear Drawings or
Sketches - but preferably with an actual Model - so that we
await same.

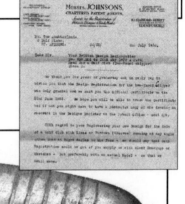

The above paragraph was taken from a letter written by Messrs. Johnsons, Chartered Patent Agents (Edinburgh), to Tom Auchterlonie, July 2, 1936.

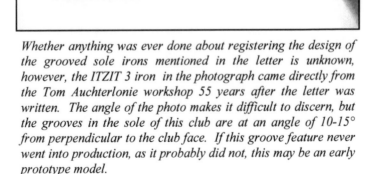

Whether anything was ever done about registering the design of the grooved sole irons mentioned in the letter is unknown, however, the ITZIT 3 iron in the photograph came directly from the Tom Auchterlonie workshop 55 years after the letter was written. The angle of the photo makes it difficult to discern, but the grooves in the sole of this club are at an angle of 10-15° from perpendicular to the club face. If this groove feature never went into production, as it probably did not, this may be an early prototype model.

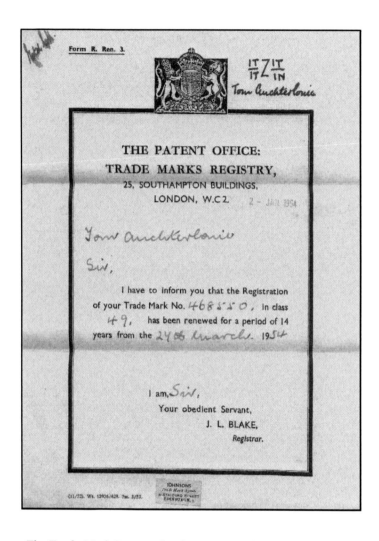

The Trade Mark Registry for the ITZIT mark in 1954. The clubs were introduced in 1926 and now, in 1954, the mark registration is in force until 1968.

Eric Auchterlonie

The period between 1925 and 1935 was very active for Tom Auchterlonie. He became well established, brought out the ITZIT line of clubs, fulfilled the Imperial Japanese orders, moved to larger quarters and witnessed the demise of his brothers' firm. One other significant event also took place in the year 1928. Tom's son, Eric, joined the firm as an apprentice.

Tom and Isabella had produced two male offspring, Norman and Eric. Norman eventually became a medical doctor. Eric would become a club maker, an exceptional club maker in time, and take over the firm. But he would earn that right and the first step was to join the works as an apprentice club maker to learn the business from the bottom up.

Eric was born in 1911. He was educated at Madras College, as was Tom Morris a century earlier, and at age 17, the time when he 'left school,' he became an apprentice like so many other young men starting into various career opportunities. The apprentice system was designed to teach a young person all about the business starting with a task as menial as sweeping the floors before climbing to the next rung on the skills ladder. In a club maker's shop, an apprenticeship may have lasted between five and seven years before a man was considered a true club maker. Eric started when Tom's shop was still on Ellice Place and he probably had completed his apprenticeship by the time the business moved to its larger space at Pilmour Links-Golf Place in 1934.

An apprentice club maker would have spent time learning each of the tasks associated with club making. They

184

A young boy , possibly Eric, playing golf in the street, perhaps in Southfield, near the old Tom Auchterlonie workshop on Fleming Place. Many boys in golf-rich St Andrews learned the same way—using the poles of street lamps as their targets.

Eric, in the pram, and his older brother, Norman.

185

included turning wood heads on a copying lathe, turning shafts from square to round on a lathe, routing wood heads for sole plates and inserts, shafting woods and irons to assure the proper lie, gripping and finishing clubs. There was also the business side of things, especially for the son of the owner.

He worked the business faithfully, helping his father build a very successful trade. In 1955 Tom made Eric a full partner and the firm became Tom Auchterlonie and Son. Tom Auchterlonie passed away in 1962 and Eric became sole proprietor of the firm, then in it's 43rd year

In 1982 he was accorded an indirect honor when His Holiness, Pope John Paul was presented with an Auchterlonie putter during his visit to Scotland. The wood shaft-wood head club was made in the Tom Auchterlonie shop and was gift indicative of Scottish culture, celebrating the Holy Father's visit.

Eric and his wife, Alice, raised two children, Avril and Keith, the latter being invaluable in the assembly of information for this volume. Although Keith did not follow in the club making footsteps of his father, grandfather and uncles, he did spend time working in the shop. The family home was over the shop and thus he grew up in the midst of the Home of Golf, in the epicenter of what was once the heart of the golf club making world.

Eric was also a keen golfer and played regularly as a member of the St Andrews Golf Club and later with Crail Golfing Society. He and his good friend, St Andrews wine merchant Willie Birrell, usually had a 9:00 tee time at Crail on Sunday morning. Even in retirement, living in Pitscottie, outside St Andrews, Eric's primary pursuits were tending to his garden and tinkering with golf clubs in

Eric Auchterlonie, the club maker, standing in front of a building that may be the firm's shop at the first tee of the Eden course. The club he is holding has a steel shaft (legalized in Britain in 1929).

A group of young club makers, probably apprentices. Eric Auchterlonie is second from left. His apprenticeship started in 1928 so this photo most likely is from the early 1930s.

his work shed. He continued to make modern copies of old brassies and wood putters, his favorite clubs.

Eric's Hstorical Knowledge

One example of Eric's great assistance with my early information gathering, and an indication of how much of the history of club making may already be lost from years of public disinterest, was the matter of a simple cleek mark. That particular mark, now known by collectors as the Tom Stewart reject mark, was on an iron club head in the Auchterlonie shop one day during one of my visits. I had seen the mark before but in the infancy of collecting old clubs, there was within collecting circles, no knowledge of its origin. Eric readily identified it and followed with this story.

> *"When we were kids, we used to go to Stewart's works and buy those rejected heads for a half crown. Then we'd take them to another maker [since Eric's family was in the business we can be pretty sure where he went] to have them shafted. If there were no imperfect heads lying about, Stewart's men would mark a good head as a reject and pocket the money for drink."*

Over twenty years later I have yet to see an explanatory reference to that mark, anywhere. Eric not only contributed that bit of information to future collectors and historians but reinforced the knowledge that Stewart works shafted no clubs, being the makers of iron heads exclusively.

D & W Auchterlonie 2-iron by Tom Stewart with two reject marks in the oval.

A Tom Auchterlonie display ad from a 1978 St. Andrews town guide. Their dedication to a quality and hand crafted product is still apparent.

PLAY

TOM AUCHTERLONIE'S

HAND CRAFTED GOLF CLUBS
Made to Measure and Specification

We have possibly the Finest Display and Selection of GOLF EQUIPMENT in Scotland.

TOM AUCHTERLONIE & SON

2/4 Golf Place, 1/2 Pilmour Links, Corner Shop, St. Andrews
Telephone 3253

Everything for the Game
Postal and Overseas Enquiries given special attention

Eric Auchterlonie , The Employer

Any customer visiting the shop in between the early 1970s and the early 1990s may very well have been served by Jim Horsfield. Jim was involved in everything from club repairing to fitting pullovers. He probably knew Eric as well as anyone else in St Andrews, having worked along side him for over 20 years.

I first new Eric when I came to live in Crail in 1971 having spent the previous 13 years in Nigeria. I met him through my Father-in-Law, Jim Mackie, who worked with Eric primarily as book-keeper but also helping in the shop. When in St Andrews I would visit and became quite friendly with Eric and, on many occasions, would join with him in his regular Sunday morning game of golf at Balcomie along with his great pal Willie Birrell [proprietor of Birrell Wine Merchants and Grocer in South Street, St Andrews]. The golf wasn't all that brilliant but the chat and the stories about St Andrews and their youth certainly made up for it.

In mid – 1975 father-in-law Jim decided to retire and concentrate on his part time job as Secretary to Crail Golfing Society. At the time I was self-employed as a retail baker in Crail, which really wasn't giving enough employment for both myself and my wife so I called in to see Eric about the job that was soon to become available. I was not only a keen golfer but had been involved in golf club management on a voluntary basis whilst in Nigeria and, as an amateur woodworker, would take on a considerable amount of golf club repair work so I was no stranger to the golf industry. Eric agreed to take me on to not only keep the firm's books but to help with the shop management for the magnificent sum of £50.00 per week!

I soon found my feet in the shop and the book-keeping side was reasonably simple so I had a lot of time to spend on the shop management side and, with Eric's permission began to

make a number of alterations to the fabric of the premises and improve the display facilities. The premises themselves were quite fascinating - 2 Golf Place having during the late 19th and early 20th centuries been the St Andrews Golf Clubhouse prior to Tom Auchterlonie taking it over and 4 Golf Place had been McArthur's bakery, shop, tearoom and, upstairs, reception rooms with a dance floor!

It was during some of my forays into the cellar under the original shop and into the roof space above the newer part of the shop that I found a veritable treasure trove of old golf clubs, heads, shafts, balls and other equipment that had been pushed into boxes, cupboards etc. Eric really did not know just what there was hidden away and I suggested that we bring them all into the shop and look at the possibility of displaying them in some way. During the winter of that year we spent much of our time sorting out all the antique clubs, we decided that the easiest and most convenient way to display them was on the ceiling of the newer [No 4] part of the shop as this ceiling was lower [but not too low] and they would be easier to see. So we fastened wooden batons to the ceiling and hung the clubs from pot hooks - wiring some the more valuable ones to the hooks so they couldn't be taken.

Eric was a mine of information about all these clubs not only about the methods of manufacture but about the men who had made them all those years ago and he seemed to have a story for every one and, looking back, I only wish I had been able to record our conversations. It was during these months that my interest in the making of and the history of club making was well and truly fired and Eric was at his most animated when he was talking about and describing the way they had been made – he would drag me down to the workshop and grab an old club head or hickory shaft to demonstrate exactly how a touch of a scraper or file on a head or a wipe with sandpaper on a shaft could change a club's characteristics immeasurably, his eyes would gleam and he would ask me questions to make sure I was listening! Sandy Smith, our club maker at the time, would stand back and smile but even he could get carried away and admitted

The ceiling of the Tom Auchterlonie shop was, at one time, a veritable club museum. In the years after this picture was taken in 1978, Eric slowly removed clubs to prevent loss from theft.

that Eric was the most knowledgeable in the art of golf club making.

There was one other – and he lived within yards – cousin Laurie! I soon learned of the situation there, they never spoke, hadn't a good word for each other and yet were the most famous names in St Andrews. I met Laurie on a number of occasions – I got sent round with mis-delivered mail etc.! He was a friendly and polite man and got as excited as Eric about golf club making but the meetings were uncomfortable because of the feud, when I got back Eric would spend the next hour asking all sorts of questions about the Old B**. I just thought it was a pity they couldn't have joined forces and given the golf world the benefit of their combined expertise.

My abiding memory of Eric was his mischievous ways he used to handle the numerous salesmen - the addition of the old clubs to the ceiling of the shop greatly aided this. In would come this bright young man with his firm's newest set of sticks "Now Mr Auchterlonie" he would say "We have revolutionised the art of club making" and I would creep into the back ground so he wouldn't see my face. The salesman would proceed to explain to a silent Eric how they had taken all the weight from the back of the club head and concentrated it into the sole and around the periphery, shortened the hosel etc. etc. etc. Having heard him out Eric would turn to me and ask me "Reach the Maxwell for me Jim " [being well over six feet I was useful for this] He would then explain in great detail how a manufacturer in eighteen ninety something had made club heads where all the weight had been transferred from the back of the club into the sole and around the edges and so on...... The poor fellow would leave suitably cowed by his meeting with the master and Eric would turn to me with a glint in his eye and the beginnings of a rare smile –"Best thing you ever did getting these old clubs down".

After that there were a number of occasions when being given the sales talk that I have reached for an old club to be told that 'I was getting as bad as Eric' and I felt complimented!

Jim Horsfield

This photo was taken on the occasion of the grand reopening of the Tom Auchterlonie & Son shop after the modernisation of 1970. Jim Horsfield is the tall gent on the left end standing next to Eric. Keith Auchterlonie is the young man in the center.

193

A display in the window of the Tom Auchterlonie shop exhibits antique clubs and the tools used to make them by hand. Jim Horsfield recalls setting up this display in 1982. The club at the far right side is a Holing Out Putter resting atop one of its advertising broadsides (see page 124).

Parcel ribbon and bits and pieces of paper from the time the Tom Auchterlonie shop was still the center of St Andrews retail golf world.

Eric Auchterlonie, typically attired in his shop coat, with Bryan Georgiady, October, 1982. Although Eric was an accomplished businessman his true passion was to tinker with clubs at the workbench.

Grandson and grandfather: Alasdair and Eric Auchterlonie, 1990.

195

1925 Tom Auchterlonie retail catalog

ALL CLUBS ARE HAND MADE

"De Luxe" Wooden Clubs

PRICES

	GENT'S	LADIES
DRIVERS		
BRASSIES		
BRASSY SPOONS		
BRASSY CLEEKS		
PLIG BRASSIES		
WOODEN PUTTERS		

"DE LUXE" DRIVER

All Hand Made by Highly Skilled Club Makers from specially selected Straight Grained Hickory and Best Quality Persimmon, fitted with Superior Calfskin or "T.A." Special Grips.

TOM AUCHTERLONIE, *Golf Club Maker*, 2 ELLICE PLACE, ST. ANDREWS

1925 Tom Auchterlonie retail catalog

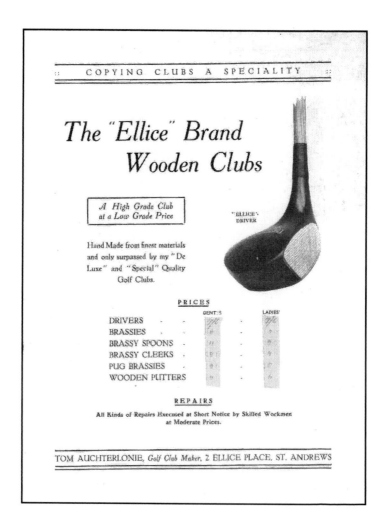

Two Tom Auchterlonie catalogs are pictured here dating from 1925 and 1927. Only the cover and two pages from the 1925 catalog are included but the entire 1927 catalog is portrayed.

The first page of the 1925 catalog shows the De Luxe model woods of that year. The are finished in a single color as opposed to the same models two years later which now have been given a tripe-top finish. Tom Auchterlonie called it "bars" rather than a stripe.

The second page shows the Tom Auchterlonie Ellice line which he labeled "A High Grade Club at a Low Grade Price." By 1928 the Ellice line had disappeared.

The 1927 catalog featured the new line of premium clubs, the ITZIT series. But more importantly it also offered steel shafted clubs two years before the Royal & Ancient Golf Club permitted their use in competition. Obviously, more Brits were beginning to use the clubs which had been accepted in the United States for three years in anticipation on the R&A lifting its ban. Tom also had many export customers in the U.S.

1927 Tom Auchterlonie retail catalog

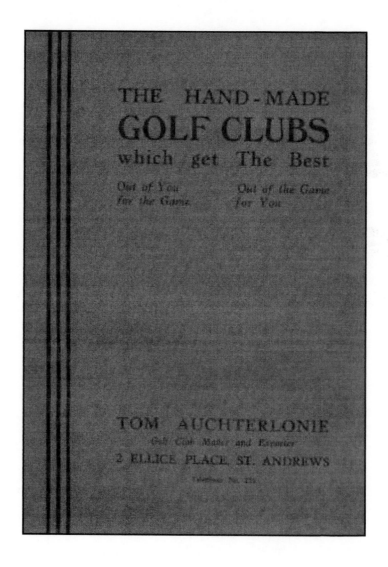

PATRONISED BY THE JAPANESE IMPERIAL FAMILY.

Work: FLEMING PLACE,
St. Andrews,
Fife.

2 Bruce Place,
St. Andrews.
Telephone No. 263.

My Claim For My Clubs.

Ladies and Gentlemen,

In presenting to you this Catalogue,
I do so with confidence and pleasure.

The Clubs I have to offer you satisfy me
as I am sure they will satisfy you. I claim their
excellence because

(1) I have played golf all my life, and I know
what is wanted in a golf club.

(2) I have spent thirty-five years giving
individual attention to the requirements of
golfers and to the construction of golf clubs.

(3) My Clubmakers are themselves golfers, and
at the same time highly expert tradesmen.

(4) I see to it, personally, that none but the
best and thoroughly seasoned material is
used in the manufacture of my clubs.

(5) Each club is hand-made, and with the
object that not only will it give the player
every assistance in playing the shot, but it
will also see that the player gets everything
that can be got out of the shot.

I ask you to accept my best thanks for past
favours, and I can assure you that my personal
attention will be given to your valued custom.

Yours very sincerely,

TOM AUCHTERLONIE.

1927 Tom Auchterlonie retail catalog

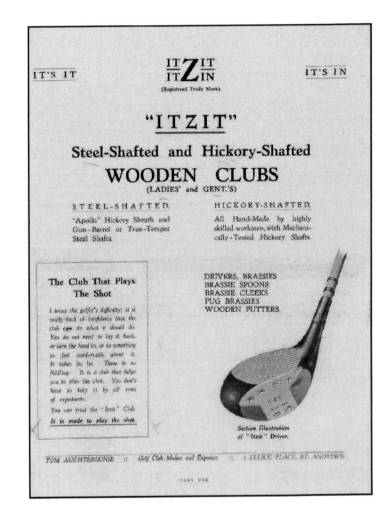

"DE-LUXE"
Steel - Shafted
Wooden Clubs
(LADIES' and GENT.'S)

With "Apollo" Gun-Barrel Finish or True - Temper Shafts.

DRIVERS
BRASSIES
BRASSIE SPOONS
BRASSIE CLEEKS
PUG BRASSIES
WOODEN PUTTERS

All Made by Highly Skilled Club Makers in my own Workshops.

Section Illustration of "De-Luxe" Steel-Shafted Driver.

TOM AUCHTERLONIE :: Golf Club Maker and Exporter :: 2 ELLICE PLACE, ST. ANDREWS

203

Peter Georgiady

1927 Tom Auchterlonie retail catalog

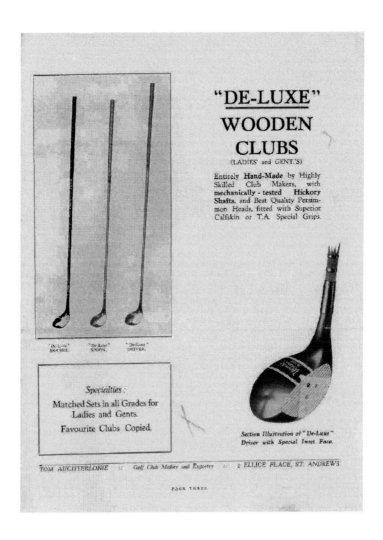

204

The "Tom Auchterlonie"
WOODEN PUTTER
A Club Which All Golfers Will Appreciate

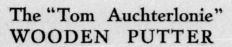

THE Heads are made from thoroughly seasoned Persimmon—the very finest procurable—and, fitted with mechanically-tested Hickory Shafts, these Putters—hand-made throughout by the most highly skilled craftsmen in the Home of Golf—constitute the highest achievement ever attained in the Golf Clubmaking World. Their beauty of finish, modern shape and perfect balance are their outstanding features.

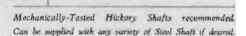

Mechanically-Tested Hickory Shafts recommended. Can be supplied with any variety of Steel Shaft if desired.

Whose Putters send the ball most true
And pile up hole on hole for you,
By sinking putts right out of view? —

TOM AUCHTERLONIE'S!

TOM AUCHTERLONIE :: Golf Club Maker and Exporter :: 2 ELLICE PLACE, ST. ANDREWS

1927 Tom Auchterlonie retail catalog

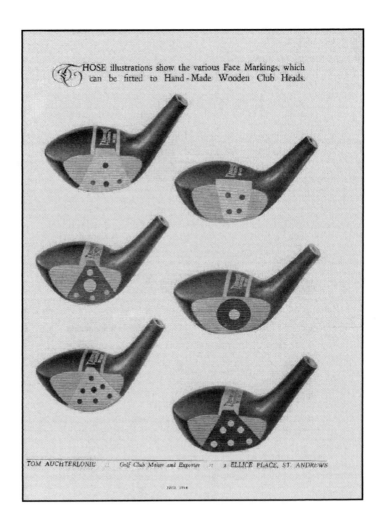

THOSE illustrations show the various Face Markings, which can be fitted to Hand-Made Wooden Club Heads.

TOM AUCHTERLONIE :: Golf Club Maker and Exporter :: 2 ELLICE PLACE, ST. ANDREWS

**IT'S
IT**

$\dfrac{\text{IT}}{\text{IT}}\text{Z}\dfrac{\text{IT}}{\text{IN}}$

(Registered Trade Mark).

Iron Clubs
(DESIGN REGISTERED)

FEATURES:

Prevent digging, allowing un-interrupted follow through.

Prevent ball from being hacked, though topped.

Prevent slipping on toe or heel of club.

Provide good sighting line and make direction easy.

Impart quick stop or underspin.

Mechanically-Tested Hickory Shafts advised, but any variety of Steel Shaft can be supplied.

Illustrations show an I T Z I T No. 3 Iron Head from different angles.

Patented

TOM A

ST

1927 Tom Auchterlonie retail catalog

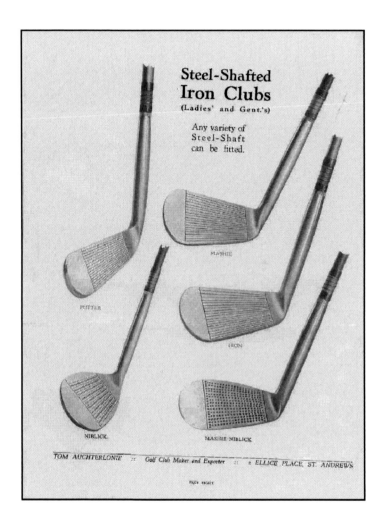

**Steel-Shafted
Iron Clubs**
(Ladies' and Gent.'s)

Any variety of
Steel-Shaft
can be fitted.

MASHIE

PUTTER

IRON

NIBLICK

MASHIE NIBLICK

TOM AUCHTERLONIE :: Golf Club Maker and Exporter :: : ELLICE PLACE, ST. ANDREWS

PAGE EIGHT

209

1927 Tom Auchterlonie retail catalog

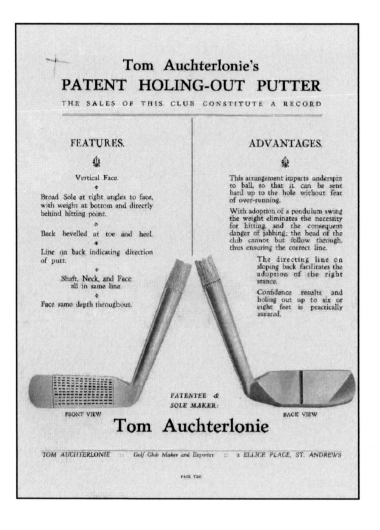

Tom Auchterlonie's
PATENT HOLING-OUT PUTTER

THE SALES OF THIS CLUB CONSTITUTE A RECORD

FEATURES.

Vertical Face.

Broad Sole at right angles to face, with weight at bottom and directly behind hitting point.

Back bevelled at toe and heel.

Line on back indicating direction of putt.

Shaft, Neck, and Face all in same line.

Face same depth throughout.

ADVANTAGES.

This arrangement imparts underspin to ball, so that it can be sent hard up to the hole without fear of over-running.

With adoption of a pendulum swing the weight eliminates the necessity for hitting, and the consequent danger of jabbing; the head of the club cannot but follow through, thus ensuring the correct line.

The directing line on sloping back facilitates the adoption of the right stance.

Confidence results and holing out up to six or eight feet is practically assured.

PATENTEE & SOLE MAKER:

FRONT VIEW   BACK VIEW

Tom Auchterlonie

TOM AUCHTERLONIE :: Golf Club Maker and Exporter :: 2 ELLICE PLACE, ST. ANDREWS

PAGE TEN

1927 Tom Auchterlonie retail catalog

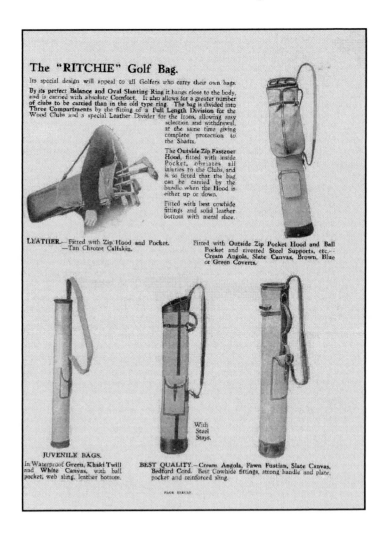

The "RITCHIE" Golf Bag.

Its special design will appeal to all Golfers who carry their own bags.

By its perfect **Balance** and **Oval Slanting Ring** it hangs close to the body, and is carried with absolute Comfort. It also allows for a greater number of clubs to be carried than in the old type ring. The bag is divided into **Three Compartments** by the fitting of a **Full Length Division** for the Wood Clubs and a special Leather Divider for the Irons, allowing easy selection and withdrawal, at the same time giving complete protection to the Shafts.

The **Outside Zip Fastener Hood**, fitted with inside Pocket, obviates all injuries to the Clubs, and is so fitted that the bag can be carried by the handle when the Hood is either up or down.

Fitted with best cowhide fittings and solid leather bottom with metal shoe.

LEATHER.—Fitted with Zip Hood and Pocket.
    —Tan Chrome Calfskin.

Fitted with Outside Zip Pocket Hood and Ball Pocket and rivetted Steel Supports, etc.—Cream Angola, Slate Canvas, Brown, Blue or Green Coverts.

With Steel Stays.

JUVENILE BAGS.
In Waterproof Green, Khaki Twill and White Canvas, with ball pocket, web sling, leather bottom.

BEST QUALITY.—Cream Angola, Fawn Fustian, Slate Canvas, Bedford Cord. Best Cowhide fittings, strong handle and plate, pocket and reinforced sling.

PAGE ELEVEN

212

"Ellice" Brand Clubs

For those who wish a cheaper priced club our *"Ellice"*
Brand is a High Grade Club at the Low Grade
Price of 10/6 each.

SUNDRIES

Persimmon
Golf Heads
Drivers, Brassies and Spoons (any pattern).
Rough Turned,
Off Scraper,
Off Sandpaper,
Stained and Finished, with or without Bars
across head.

Hickory
Golf Shafts
Suppled in First, Second or Third qualities,
finished, with Grips, or in any stage from the
Rough Turned Shaft.

Steel Shafts   Any variety at makers' prices.

Golf Grips   The "T.A" Tacky, Calfskin Grip, Red or
Black, Ordinary Calfskin, Chrome and Holdfast
Grips.

Golfing
Umbrellas
At popular prices, according to size and
quality.

Grip Wax, Caddie Polish, Tees (all kinds),
Jade Tape, Golf Club Head Covers (various),
Golf Ball Cleaners, Practice Golf Balls, Club
Separators, Golfing Gloves, Campbell Grips,
Gripolin, Golfing Jackets, etc., etc.

Golf Balls   All popular makes at standard prices.

The Auchterlonie Shops — 2006

Throughout this book period photos show the various Auchterlonie shops and retail premises as they once were. Most of those same buildings exist today though several have changed functions and all have been updated.

Below: 9 Union Street, the Auchterlonie family home from the mid-19th century. Here David Auchterlonie raised his six sons and two daughters. Willie lived here for a while,

too, until he moved to 3 Pilmour Links. The elder David ran his plumbing business from the workshop adjacent to the house and that workshop also served David and Willie in their club making business.

146 North Street: This building housed the first shop belonging to Auchterlonie & Crosthwaite in 1893. Today the shop window has been removed and replaced with a more residential window—because the premises are now a residence.

Albany Place and Ellice Place: buildings on the left side of the street are Albany, on the right Ellice. The original D&W shop was by the small white sign on left, the original Tom shop was opposite the second car on the right.

Top: 4 Pilmour Links: In 1899 D&W moved to this shop. The windows and woodwork have been updated, otherwise much is the same now as then. Bottom: The D & W shop was next door to Robert Forgan's shop and works (white building). Later the Forgan works became the famous St. Andrews Woolen Mill. That was the rear entrance, the front faced the links. The Forgan name, in brass letters, was once in the pavement, now it adorns the links side wall of the building.

3 Pilmour Links: The entrance to the first floor (upstairs) residence of David Auchterlonie's family, later Willie and finally Laurie, next door to the shop. Recently a plaque was mounted next to the entryway commemorating the business and golf exploits of Willie Auchterlonie and his son, Laurie.

2 Ellice Place: The first retail location of Tom Auchterlonie, beginning in 1919. The building is essentially the same but the modern glazing belies the fact that Tom's business started over 85 years ago.

In the lower photo, 2 Ellice Place is located far left. The shop called Harbour House is at 5 Ellice Place. It was formerly the site of D. Anderson & Sons, club makers, and their shop.

Top: 1-2 Pilmour Links, the location where Tom moved his shop in 1934. His residence was above the shop, accessed through the door in the center.

Bottom: A view of the 1 Pilmour Links and the 4 Golf Place entrances. Tom frequently referred to his business as "The Corner Shop," because that's what it was and it also distinguished him from his brothers' business, which was not on a corner.

2-4 Golf Place, the side entrance of the Tom Auchterlonie shop, eventually used as the main entrance since Golf Place was the street that ran down to the links. The form of the building is totally intact with the woodwork around the windows and doors being refreshed.

Also see The Corner Shop on pages 19 and 143.

Index

David, Willie, Tom and Eric Auchterlonie are not listed in the index because their names appear so frequently.